GENESIS

A JOURNEY OF BECOMING NEW AND TURNING FROM SHAME TO PRIDE

JORDAN ROBERTS

Book Design by HMDpublishing

ISBN: 979-8-9882488-2-8

Author's Note

This book is dedicated to my parents who raised me with love, despite our differences. I also dedicate this book to those individuals in the LGBTQ+ community who feel lost and confused.

Conversations and stories have been re-created from my memory to the best of my ability to convey their significance in my life. Some names have been changed to protect the identity of those discussed throughout this work.

I hope by reading my story, you will be encouraged to tell your own.

I originally wrote my memoir, Genesis, with the hope to reach an LGBTQ+ audience who wrestled with their sexual identity like I did. I wanted to expose the mental health traumas that result from not being accepted for who you are. People shouldn't have to choose between their sexuality and their relationship with God. God loves you the same whether you identify as gay or straight. Growing up, I had to choose one or the other, and that choice almost cost me my life.

After the events of near tragedy, I realized that the only choice I had to make was whether or not I believed in God because His love transcends how I identify as a person. And that realization changed everything.

After writing my original memoir, holding it my hands and reading it cover to cover, a flood of thoughts and inspiration came over me that I wanted to share with you, the reader. So, I have adapted this version to include those thoughts to provide a more relatable story. As humans, we evolve and learn as we walk through our journey; it's okay to change. We must share these teachings with others, and that's what I want to do with you.

If you've read the original version, I thank you for your support, and I hope that you enjoyed it and it benefited you. This new version will include most of the original text as well as additional chapters and stories to help those like me live the life they deserve to live.

Introduction

There comes a point in our lives when we decide who we want to be. And that choice will not please everyone. In our deciding, we must consider the following—are we choosing our happiness or the happiness of others?

When I was a kid—about five or six years old—I had a gold-blonde, shoulder-length wig that was left over from Halloween that year; it was 1996. The faux hair was tangled and knotted; even though the netting on the cap was starting to come apart, I loved to wear it. Sometimes I'd take the 101 Dalmatian comforter off of my bed and wrap it around my body as if it were a magnificent ball gown. I'd twirl around my room, feeling like a beautiful princess.

This early recollection (and others like it) serves as a window to see where my journey began. All I really wanted was to be accepted. But I was different; I knew it, and the world knew it. I didn't fit in with the other boys because I preferred decorating cakes, singing musical theater and trying on dresses over playing sports. And this kind of diversity identified as a problem.

Playing dress up as a little boy didn't feel wrong, rather, it felt comfortable. What I didn't realize then was how such innocent play would bear complicated outcomes, confusion and crisis later on.

I spent twenty-six years hiding, working tirelessly to be the biblical man everyone expected me to be. But I never hit the mark because there was this war raging within me, a sinful desire completely contradicting what I had dedicated my life to—the pursuit of holiness. What would others think of me?

The thing we have to understand is that it's okay if others don't agree with our decisions. It's impossible to appease everyone. But if you're like me, then people-pleasing is a major part of your personality and mentality. The key is to break that habit because the people you're trying to please aren't living your life. Their ability to thrive and be happy should not be rooted in your suffering. You have to own your happiness. You were created uniquely to be exactly who you are. Don't let someone else's version of who they think you should be dictate who you become. Bottom line: you're going to offend someone no matter how hard you try to please everyone.

If you're like me, then I'll bet that you've felt like a failure at some point in your life. Or perhaps you have asked the question, *what is my purpose in this life?* For me, I'd never felt like I belonged. And this feeling of being an outsider was based on the fact that I did not and could not seem to measure up to the standard that was set for me by the church. The standard was living a pious and pure life. Maybe your standard was different, but the principle remains clear. I fell through the cracks as my sexual identity clashed with the Christian principles that formed my worldview.

Like any good church boy, I wanted nothing more than to make my parents proud. And I believe that on a professional level I have done that. But on a spiritual level, I was never able to hit the mark that every Christian parent wants for their child. I was born with a nasty sin, like a disease, that poisoned the familial relationship.

This isn't a story of blame. It isn't a story of defamation or finger pointing. Love was never a question in my family, for which I'm grateful. But when someone says they love you but can't accept you, the latter discredits the former. What is love without acceptance? To me, it feels like emptiness. But I wanted resolution. I wanted to be accepted, but acceptance couldn't be granted in good conscience as set forth by the biblical truths such as homosexuals will not inherit the kingdom of God.

The following pages will serve as a detailed account of my battle with mental health and the sexual identity crisis that brought me to the point of questioning the validity of God and my place in this world. This book is for LGBTQ+ individuals trying to find their purposes in life, for those searching to find God through their struggles, and for anyone seeking hope in their war with mental health, depression, anxiety, sexual orientation, or thoughts of suicide. This is my story of growing up gay in an evangelical environment. It's my story of tragedy and redemption, one of struggle and hope, written as a guide to help those dealing with the same frustrations and anxiety I was and learn how to live with them. I want you to find peace wherever you're at in life.

My story is a testament that you aren't alone in your fight and that there is hope for you. God doesn't make mistakes. Therefore, I am not a mistake. And neither are you. You are not a problem; and you don't need to change.

PART
One

Chapter One

Whether or not I would live or die came down to one pivotal moment. The night was dark and the late November air was chilly. *Would anyone miss me?* I thought as I walked briskly to my apartment in the northside of Chicago. I breathed the cold air in, which felt like ice entering my lungs. I was alive, but I felt a hollow void in places I can only imagine.

I'd thought about suicide a hundred times, but I never got as close until now. When I arrived home, the warmth welcomed me as I let out a sigh of relief. I opened up a bottle chardonnay, my constant friend. *Men just want me for sex.* I thought. And I gave it to them. I gave anything to not feel alone. But the things I did to make me feel connected to others, left me lonelier than ever. *Where was my place in this world? Did I have a place in it?* I felt like a mistake.

Why would God do this to me? I prayed as if someone were listening.

I felt that God didn't like me. I was like that friend who always wanted to play but was ignored. God felt silent. The Creator of all things; the Designer of me and everyone gave me a thorn in my flesh, a cross to bear. But I didn't bear the cross; it bore me.

My entire childhood and early adult life were spent dedicating my life to being a faithful disciple, but it felt vain. What was supposed to work, didn't. I sought God, but I didn't find him like the Bible said I would. I prayed a book's worth, but where are those pleas now? God had failed me. And if God fails you, well, what else is there to do?

I was thirty years old, and I had lost all hope. It was as if God gave up on me. Then again, had there ever been a time when I had felt connected to God and to myself?

One morning, when I was about seven years old, I came bursting out of my room, ran down the hall and into the kitchen where my mom was making breakfast. The pancakes on the skillet were starting to bubble as the bacon sizzled, cracked and popped. My mom looked at me from where she was standing at the stove, waiting to hear what the fuss was about. "I just got saved!" I exclaimed with excitement. "Oh, that is wonderful, honey!" She proclaimed with a smile on her face. "Now, you need to live like you're saved." She said with a serious, but caring tone. I knew what she meant. Being saved meant obeying the Bible and being holy. A few weeks later, I was baptized in front of our entire church at the quarterly baptismal service that took place at a park on Lake Michigan. Thus, started my spiritual journey and warfare.

In the Roberts household, there was one decree above all else: honor and glorify God in everything. To remind us of that, we had a piece of art that was proudly displayed in the living room, which said, "As for me and my house, we will serve the Lord." And that's the law we lived by.

Everything we did was centered around the Bible. When my siblings and I got in trouble, my mom would hand us a piece of paper and tell us to write out a Bible verse twenty times. It was usually a verse about why we got into trouble, but the generic one was "Children, obey your parents in the Lord, for this is right." Ephesians 6:1

I grew up Baptist. Every time the church doors were open, we were there. The earliest church experience I remember was at the age of six. My family and I attended Bark River Bible Church in the Upper Peninsula of Michigan, where I was born. I loved going to church, singing the hymns, participating in Sunday school, engaging in children's activities (like AWANA), and, my personal favorite, attending the potluck dinners.

Christian values cradled my childhood; my parents reinforced these principles through rules on music and TV as well as our dedicated church attendance, church involvement, and the Christian education they sacrificed for us to have. It was through these mediums that I was taught that being gay is a choice. In fact, it is a sin. And choosing to be gay would be yielding to living a sinful lifestyle outside the will of God.

If you couldn't already tell, my parents were devout Christians, and they were dedicated to consistency. They didn't just read the Bible— they modeled their lives after Christ. They took what was written, "Be in the world, not of the world," seriously and engrained this same biblical framework into us kids. My parents didn't grow up in a Christian environment. They knew the cruelties and harsh realities of the world. So they wanted to protect us from the temptations they knew could cause us to sin. The irony, though, is that the protection provided served as a catalyst for agony, which will unfold through this story.

The Bible was black and white and everything centered around salvation in our Christian circles. Either you're going to heaven, or you're going to hell. Either you're saved or you aren't. Either you're doing wrong or you aren't. Who would want to go to hell? So I understood that the only way to make it to heaven was by trusting in Jesus as my Savior from sin. And the way I did that was to invite him into my heart. But it never felt quite right. There was so much importance around salvation and the sinner's prayer that I was afraid to mess it up. Did I use the right words? Was my intent genuine enough? Did I have enough faith? I'd get so paranoid about doing it wrong that I'd say the sinner's prayer multiple times on many different occasions to make sure I was going to the right place. It was a lot to put my whole life and destiny into the faith of a prayer, and I just wanted it to work. But I always felt like something was missing. I didn't feel like a Christian.

Salvation was accompanied by some miraculous work or transformative experience. I'd sit in church and listen as members told their redemption testimony. It was always about how they lived terrible lives of sin and debauchery, headed straight for Hell. Then, one day, God called them to salvation, they prayed the sinner's prayer and immediately felt the weight of their sin vanish as they gave their heart to Jesus. The congregation would applaud as some shouted an "amen" to voice their approval. The stories were emotional and moving. Some people would say that they felt an immediate transformation and claimed to be a brand-new person echoing the verse in 2 Corinthians that says all those who are in Christ are a new creature and old things have passed away. Other people would say their transformation happened over a longer period, but they no longer found pleasure doing sinful things.

I didn't have that experience. I didn't have a story that moved people to tears. Did I need one to really be saved? I thought that being saved meant you had some emotional revolution that turned you from sin into righteousness. Because that's what I witnessed and that's what happened to my parents. I grew up in a Christian home, so my testimony was just a prayer. And I wasn't sure that was enough.

My parents taught us to be a light in this dark world. They weren't ashamed of the Gospel. One of the things I respected most about my parents was their consistency to Christian living. They didn't cherry pick from the Bible; it was all or nothing. And while this lifestyle created a strict, biblical environment, hypocrisy took no place in my parents' lives. Consistency is a powerful tool that builds respect and trust.

We were the type of family that prayed in public. I loved going out to eat growing up, as most kids do. But I knew that eating in a restaurant also meant that the time would come for us to bow our heads and pray. For me, I didn't mind praying and talking about the Bible at home, where no one could see or hear us, but it felt quite embarrassing when people noticed our religious habits. I didn't want to be different. I was afraid of not fitting in. And perhaps that fear came from the realization that deep down I knew that I was different, which was scary. Furthermore, I didn't want others to look at us and judge us. I received enough judgement from my peers and siblings for being effeminate; I didn't want to give people another reason to stare.

One evening my parents took us all out to the local Cracker Barrel. It was a family favorite not only because the food was tasty, but also because all of the games to play and knickknacks to sift through occupied our time while we waited for our meal to come.

As we entered the restaurant, the hostess gathered up six menus and guided us over to where we would be sitting, which just so happened to be right next to a checkerboard near a fireplace that had a few fresh logs burning.

We took our seats and scoured the menu to find our favorite dishes. For me, it was always chicken tenders, fries, and mac and cheese with a side of BBQ sauce. The waiter came to our table and introduced himself and welcomed us into the restaurant before taking our orders. When he left, my dad lifted his voice and motioned us to fold our hand and bow our heads to pray. Reluctantly, I bowed my head before I gave a quick scan around the room to see if anyone was watching. I'd hoped that my dad would say a quick prayer before the waiter came back. But to my terror, the waiter returned to our table midprayer with a tray full of drinks. I silently looked up and locked eyes with him before I returned my gaze back down to the floor. He waited there patiently as my dad finished saying grace.

I felt so embarrassed. *Why did we always have to pray in public? This long, drawn-out prayer is causing other people to wait on us*, I thought.

As my dad said amen, the waiter started to pass out the drinks. And when he got to mine, I looked at him again, and he gave me a quick wink telling me it was okay. I took a big gulp of water and then rushed over to challenge my brother in a game of checkers as we waited for our food.

Growing up, godly music was a big part of my family. My dad often led music at church on Sundays, my sister and I took piano lessons, and my middle brother played guitar. I also loved to sing, but I kept my voice contained to the shower, until I later discovered that people might actually want to hear me sing.

My introduction to music were the old-time hymns like "Just a Closer Walk with Thee," "I'll Fly Away," "Great Is Thy Faithfulness," and the famous altar call "Come Just as You Are" among many others. But as I became older, I gained an interest in other types of music.

When I entered middle school, I learned about mainstream music from my classmates and peers as they'd talk about the latest songs and artists. Then they'd hand me one side of their headphones and we'd listen together. It felt wrong because the words were usually vulgar and definitely not Christian. I could hear my dad saying, *"Honor and glorify God in all you do."* but I wanted to keep listening. And most importantly, I wanted to fit in.

By the time I entered middle school, I'd had many crushes on a range of males, from members of boy bands to movie stars to my peers. One of my movie crushes played the prince in the live-action version of *Cinderella*. Growing up, we didn't own the movie, but we had friends who did. I remember asking to borrow the film often so I could watch it and study the prince in all his ways. I envied Cinderella as she knew what it was like to be in his arms. And she was so pretty, like I wanted to be.

I remember rummaging through my mom's closet to try on high heels, skirts, and dresses. I used clip-on earrings and washable markers as eye shadow and nail polish. A few times, I even got daring enough to open my mom's makeup bag and apply layers of eyeshadow and lipstick. I'd then thrown on that blonde wig to complete the outfit. I am sure my mom realized that her makeup was messed with, but she never brought it up, relegating this behavior as a phase. I am grateful we skipped that awkward conversation.

I enjoyed exploring something different, and I admired the person I dressed up to be. I wasn't trying to be rebellious or weird; rather, I was expressing who I was inside even before I knew what it meant. But influential people in my parents' lives noticed my peculiar choices and feminine mannerisms, so they gave their opinion on how to deal with the situation.

My family became very close with some of the leaders of the church we attended. I overheard one leader telling my parents one morning after church that they needed to get me into baseball or a similar sport to surround me with other boys to help influence a more masculine outcome. The following summer, my mom enrolled me in the community baseball league.

I didn't want to go, but my mom told me that I needed to be a part of a summer sport. And there was no room for discussion. So, I went. I didn't find the sport enjoyable because I wasn't good at it, and my teammates became upset with me when I messed up. My coordination was off, and I didn't care enough about baseball to want to get better. Furthermore, I felt like others were trying to change me, and I didn't like that. I completed the season and a few days later received word that insured I wouldn't have to play again. We were moving and the real adventure was about to start.

Chapter Two

When I was eleven years old, my parents moved us from our home in Michigan to West Virginia. My dad felt called to retire from the business world and go to college. He wanted to earn a degree in family counseling to become a therapist. So, during the summer of 2001, we packed up and moved to West Virginia.

The move was difficult on the family. We confronted a lot of change as we entered into a different culture and a completely different lifestyle. We moved into housing provided by the college for students with families. It was a frightening downsize. In Michigan, we'd enjoyed a spacious house with six bedrooms and three bathrooms, sitting on thirty-nine acres of land. In West Virginia, we occupied a three-bedroom, one-and-a-half-bath condo. Not only did we downsize in living space, but also we adjusted to being a one-income family, as my dad studied full time, and my mom worked in the kitchen at the college as a cook. I shared a bedroom with one brother while my oldest brother got his own room; my sister had just graduated high school. That fall, both my sister and my dad entered as freshmen.

Despite the drastic change, I loved living on the college campus. In the summer, there was a pool open to the community and a pond that could be used for swimming and fishing. I spent many hours flipping over rocks and searching through the water banks for frogs, salamanders, and turtles. I loved wildlife, and I enjoyed caring for and playing with the small amphibians I caught. The campus was filled with endless trails through a thick forest of trees and lush flora. It was a wonderland that cured my boredom on a daily basis.

To stick to our Christian traditions, my parents enrolled my brother and me in the local Christian school. One of the first friends I made there was Ariel Gray, who happened to live a few doors down from me. Ariel and I spent every day together running back and forth to each other's houses, finding new games to play and trails to hike. During the hot summer days, we spent the afternoons at the pool, swimming and bathing underneath the warming rays of the sun.

One day during one of our play dates Ariel told me, "Jordan, I like you."

"Oh, I like you too!" I replied with a warm smile.

"No." She said, "I like, like you."

"Oh." I looked down at the ground while my face turned red.

"Well," I started sheepishly, "I like you as a friend, and I love hanging out with you."

"I know. I like hanging out with you, too! So, why can't we be more?" she pleaded.

"I just know that I would prefer to be friends." I knew in my heart that I wasn't attracted to females, which was something I dared not voice.

The importance of gender roles was significant growing up. Being in a devout Christian family, these roles were taken seriously and interpreted as seen in the Bible. Men and women had specific functions and responsibilities. For example, boys played sports, performed manual labor, worked out, enjoyed cars, roughhoused with their friends, and liked getting dirt under their nails. In other words, boys did "manly" things. Women, on the other hand, went to the spa, had their nails done, gossiped about boys, baked, cooked, cleaned, and braided their hair. You know, women did all the "girly" stuff.

I was docile and gentle. I didn't like roughhousing with my friends or working on cars. I especially hated it when my brothers pushed me around and said, "We need to toughen you up." I wanted to learn how to bake and paint or drink tea while holding discussions about the latest music or fashion trends. I felt different from my male peers, so most of my friends growing up were girls. What I was looking for was someone to tell me that it was OK to be myself.

My dad enrolled my brother and me in a jujitsu class so we could learn self-defense. I hated every second of it. This was a full-body-contact experience where we were taught different techniques for grappling. We were then be paired off to demonstrate what we had learned. I can still smell my opponent's sweat as we wrestled to the floor, each trying to pin the other down.

The fighting used to make me so angry that I screamed inside, though it was expected that I enjoy it. Along with self-defense, I was supposed to learn how to be tougher because that's what boys did. While learning how to fight to protect yourself is good, enrolling in the class sent the wrong message that I wasn't good enough the way that I was. To me, it wasn't about learning self-defense techniques. It was an effort to change me to be more like a boy. I will not say that putting me in the class was a deliberate act to make me miserable, but I wish that my voice would have been heard. But whether or not I wanted to go wasn't up for discussion.

My brothers, on the other hand, loved the class. They couldn't wait to get on the mat. For them, the grappling improved their manliness and gave them an advantage over their friends when they engaged in friendly wrestling matching. It fed their desire of male dominance.

I dreaded the class. Some weeks I feigned illness to avoid going, which sometimes worked. People didn't understand why I didn't like it. And as a result, I felt like there was something wrong with me. *Why couldn't I be like the other boys and my brothers? Why did I have to be different?*

I had no idea who I was; I struggled on a daily basis because I was too afraid to be who I really was. So, I did everything in my power to deflect what I hated about myself.

During the summer months, I went to the community pool with Ariel almost every day. It was big and equipped with a diving board. My friends and I took turns performing front and backflips while showing off our amateur diving skills. I loved trying new and complicated dives. I once got daring enough to attempt a handstand on the edge of the diving board before I sprung off into a traditional front dive.

It was on the diving board that I discovered a love for gymnastics, so I transformed the flipping from the diving board into tumbling on the ground. One of the lifeguards (who I will call), Erin, was a cheerleader at the local high school. Having noticed my interest in gymnastics, she offered to help me learn the basics before I looked for a place to get formal training. I eagerly accepted the help, and we began working on the fundamentals that day.

I learned the basics quickly and then moved on to back handsprings. Once I learned how to do one, it was easy to keep going. I used to do a round off into six back handsprings in a row. From there, I learned how to complete a back tuck. This is where I did a backflip in midair without touching my hands to the ground.

I loved gymnastics. I practiced every day for multiple hours. I worked out to build strength in my arms and core to support my bodyweight as I attempted more complicated routines. Erin worked with me a lot, corrected my form, and remained patient with me as I advanced with her. She was nice but tough. During our practice sessions, if I messed up or looked sloppy, she would make me do ten push-ups and ten sit-ups. But I enjoyed her strict eye to detail. She wanted me to do well, and I could feel it not only in how quickly I was improving but also in the soreness of my muscles the following day.

Tumbling allowed me to create a world where I could be free. I spent most of my afternoons flipping around making up different combinations of roundoffs, back handsprings and back tucks along with other small body movements and stretches one might see at gymnastics meets. The tumbling court was my world.

After my quick advancement, Erin suggested that I enroll in the gymnastics class where she practiced. I went with her the following week. Of course, I loved it. That same day, I rushed home and enthusiastically asked my parents if I could start taking gymnastics lessons. They seemed to not mind me practicing on my own, but enrolling me in a girl-dominated sport was not going to happen. They denied my request. I was crushed. I'd finally found a sport I loved but was told it wasn't manly enough. I felt embarrassed and hurt. Here I was giving people another reason to question me. I hated it. I hated myself.

My parents noticed my feminine tendencies. I believe this instilled fear that I would turn out to be gay. Participating in gymnastics wouldn't have made me gay because I was already gay. With or without the influences they thought were bad, I was still gay. Gymnastics wouldn't change it, sports wouldn't change it, and jujitsu wouldn't change it.

To me, gymnastics wasn't about being gay. It was about finally finding something that I liked and was good at. I found something to identify with, something that allowed me to set achievable goals and be a part of a team. To me, it was about the sport; to my parents, it was about morality.

Gymnastics helped me feel like a person. The sport provided a space to funnel my stress, anger, and doubts in a way that was healthy and, in return, life-giving. But I gave it up for the sake of appearance. I searched for something to take its place.

Chapter Three

I took piano lessons growing up. My teacher was a college student who played the piano exceptionally well. He was tall, dark, and handsome. He also attended our church and helped out in the youth group, which I attended regularly. We met once a week for thirty minutes, which sometimes went longer depending on the difficulty of the songs or nature of the content being learned. Through our lessons, I developed a small crush on him.

We always began the lesson with scales and then moved right on to what I'd been working on that week. With sweat soaking my armpits, I would raise my clammy hands over the white keys as I looked at my music and began to play, often messing up and requesting to start over.

I kept telling myself that everyone gets nervous around their friends. Getting older, my attraction toward men grew. And as it grew, I became bolder in figuring out what these feelings meant.

We had one computer in the house, which was located in the living room with the screen facing toward the room so it could always be seen by anyone in the room. Despite the likely chance of getting caught, I searched websites like Abercrombie & Fitch or Hollister so I could look at the male models. And if anyone came in, I could say that I was browsing clothing items. I remember going to the mall and walking past these stores. The strong smell of cologne permeated the storefront as two male models with chiseled abs and muscular arms stood out front to engage those walking by. I'd walk by the store multiple times to get a few extra looks at the men who made my heart beat faster.

One afternoon I came home from school to an empty house. My brother was at basketball practice, my dad was studying in the library, and my mom was at work. I kicked off my shoes, threw my backpack up the stairs, and wandered over to the couch to click the TV on with the remote. Flipping through the channels, I came across the movie *American Pie*. I'd heard kids at school talk about this movie but had obviously never seen it because my parents never would have allowed us kids to watch. Being alone at home, I decided to keep the movie on with the remote in hand in case someone was to walk through the door.

Before long, the famous pie scene came on. As the scene played, I became glued to the TV. My eyes widened. I leaned forward a bit and felt my heart beating faster and faster in my chest.

Am I about to see a naked man? I thought as I watched the scene intently. As the part came to an end, I was somewhat disappointed no nudity was shown, but also confused (and scared) by how much I enjoyed watching it.

If I was a Christian, then I shouldn't be struggling the way I was. All of those warnings from the pulpit came back to me. I kept a prayer journal where I wrote down many things. One afternoon as I struggled with my feelings, I wrote about my same-sex attraction and prayed to God asking him for any other struggle than this one. I repeatedly told myself that I wasn't a homosexual and that I loved God and desired to serve him. How could I love the Lord and be a homosexual at the same time? Can the two coexist? I found comfort in the fact that I chose God over this sin that seemed to define me. I prayed for God to take the gay away from me. Then I felt a calming sense that if I were saved—I'd prayed the prayer many times—then I couldn't be a homosexual. I gave a sigh of relief while I closed my Bible and prayer journal.

Even though I struggled to identify who I was inside, my outward femininity didn't do me any favors. In school, kids often called me gay in the way that I talked and carried myself. My brothers and their friends referred to me as a "fairy" growing up. I remember one afternoon they had their friends over to the house and one of them made a comment about me being "a little fairy." Embarrassed and humiliated, I shouted back, "Well, maybe I am!" I ran up the stairs, slammed the door to my room, and hid the rest of the time they were there. I wanted to feel safe in my own home, but that wasn't possible when the discrimination was brought to my doorstep. While my parents disapproved of this behavior, the hurt from the perpetual comments took up residence in my heart. I didn't feel comfortable in an environment that didn't accept me for who I was. So I shut down and started to build a wall between my family and myself.

My brothers played basketball through high school. My parents and I went to almost every one of their games. My parents went to show their support, but I went because I liked to watch the cheerleaders cheer and tumble, especially during halftime. I actually looked forward to the games. I could care less who was winning because my focus was on the sidelines where I thought the excitement was. I even remember on occasion seeing a few male cheerleaders from the public high schools our school used to play against. How badly I wished I could be one of them as I sat their studying their cheers and even clapping along with them sometimes.

One evening, my mom asked me to clap for her as we were driving home from one of the games. I was taken aback by the odd request but clapped my hands together the way I'd seen the cheerleaders do it with hands wrapped around each other almost in a hug rather than fingers against palm.

When I mimicked the cheerleader, my mom asked me in an accusatory tone, "Why do you clap like that?"

I replied timidly, "I don't know. That's just the way I clap."

She gave me a quizzical look as the light turned green, and she gently pressed the gas pedal.

I could tell that my mom was trying to find a way to discuss this odd behavior, but I didn't feel the need to have to explain myself.

I hated my feminine side because it made me different. And it was something I couldn't hide. As I got older, I tried to be the complete opposite in hopes that I wouldn't feel so different from my peers.

~❖~

Growing up in West Virginia provided many ways to prove my masculinity. The mountainous terrain and raging rivers made it the perfect spot for extreme sports such a rock climbing, rappelling, spelunking, white water rafting, and hiking. I indulged in all of these activities. I didn't enjoy these pastimes; however, I felt like I had to do them.

The scariest sport I ever participated in was white water rafting. I was never a great swimmer, so the idea of rafting through world-class rapids was an uneasy feeling to me. But I did end up rafting the New River, not once, but twice.

Going down the river usually consists of four or five large rafts that hold nine people: eight riders and one guide. Between rapids, the guide prepares the rafters for the next rapid. He or she would tell us exactly when to paddle and, most importantly, where to swim if we fell into the water. Heeding the advice of the guide is paramount in the event one finds himself being tossed and turned by the raging rapids of the unforgiving river. Failure to swim in the right direction could end up in loss of life. Some rapids required us to row long and hard to make it through while others required little effort as we relied on the current to whisk us through as our leader skillfully guided the boat where he wanted it to go.

I will never forget one particular rapid called Keeney's. The unique position of the rocks that guided the strong current made it extremely dangerous. My heart began pounding as we approached this legendary rapid. I listened intently to what the guide had to say and repeated the instructions to myself as the river's current pushed us closer to the white, angry water ahead. Now just feet away from the rapid, my rafting partners and I waited eagerly for directions from our guide.

Then, suddenly, he began shouting, "Row! Row!" and we did with all our might.

We entered the rapid; there was no turning back. Water splashed all around us as we used our paddles to fight the strength of the waves. We kept rowing and riding, the raft ramping up one side of it and then down the other.

I can still see the guide in my periphery, leaning back intensely with his paddle to one side of the raft purposefully guiding the boat away from jagged rocks and holes that could effortlessly flip the raft over into the rapid. As the current whisked us down the river, I got that tingling sensation deep in my stomach. It's that feeling you get as you're climbing up the tracks on a roller coaster and zoom down the other side. It was terrifying but exciting.

We rode another wave as we continued to vigorously row. By this time, we were all soaked from the waves crashing over the sides of the raft. Out of nowhere came another massive wave, forcing the raft into an almost vertical position. We leaned forward and clutched the boat for dear life, praying the raft didn't flip backward into the hungry mouth of the river. We pitched forward as the front of the raft smacked the water as we all let out a sigh of relief. The wave sent a ripple through the raft as we made it to the other side of the rapid.

We had done it! We experienced an exhilarating ride, but once was enough for me.

I thought that the more adventurous things I did, the more masculine I would appear to others. But my personality, mannerisms, and so on weren't going to change just because I was hanging off the side of a cliff in a harness attached to a long rope. Through these adventures, I was looking for acceptance, but my peers weren't ready to embrace something they didn't understand.

Another effort I made to try and discourage the hateful comments was to date girls. How could my peers call me gay if I were dating women? So I intentionally went on the hunt to win girls over with my preteen charm. Most didn't buy it, but I did manage to woo one girl I dated on and off for a couple of years. We made each other laugh and thoroughly enjoyed each other's company. I gave her my first kiss as we found ourselves alone in the assembly hall of the school where we met. As we were standing there alone, the time felt right to lean in for a quick peck on the lips. That peck lead to a bigger kiss and full-on make-out sessions when I thought, *How manly am I?* But something always held me back. I didn't really want to be kissing a girl.

One of my favorite memories from this period was spending time with my friend Susan (whose real name will remain anonymous), a master cake baker. We went to the same school and the same church. She was two years older than me, but her sister was in my class. Our friendship began in the church youth group where we met every Wednesday night. She taught me everything I know about decorating and designing; we shared the most incredible time creating wonderful pieces of edible art. I felt safe within my creations, but ashamed to voice this consolation to others. Looking back, I realize now that without people like me, our world would be a lot less colorful and creative. I know God loves art and beauty because he created gay people.

Art was a great escape for me because it gave me a place to reveal my emotions in the name of creativity. It was therapeutic—a release of emotional turbulence that was otherwise kept inside. Not only did I learn a new skill, but also I was able to create something that represented a piece of myself. I decorated my cakes with a lot of color, and I used many different tips to create different designs. In a way, this variety mirrored who I was inside—maybe a little different but beautiful. And isn't that what we all want—to express ourselves?

Chapter Four

*I*n the summer of 2006, my dad graduated from college. To continue his education, my family and I moved to Clarks Summit, Pennsylvania, where my dad was accepted into a master of counseling program.

We moved there the summer before I started my junior year of high school. My sister had graduated from college, my oldest brother was in college, and my second-oldest brother was still living at home.

A couple weeks before school started, I remember my mom and brother encouraged me to look into sports opportunities at my new school. I believe they continued to adopt this idea that if I were involved in sports (masculine sports in their minds), then I would forsake my feminine tendencies and finally be the man they wanted me to be.

For days, they incessantly cheered me toward trying out for the soccer team. Reluctantly, I finally agreed to attend a meeting for those participating in the soccer tryouts. I wanted to please my family, so I went and tried, which is more than I had done in previous years. I made the team. And I didn't make the team because I was good; rather, they needed players. I didn't particularly love soccer, but there were some highlights to playing on the team.

First, it kept me in great shape, and I did enjoy the regular, organized workout that the whole team and I did together. I built endurance from running. It kept me healthy not only physically but also mentally. I learned to channel some of my frustrations and anxiety into exercise.

Second, I wasn't the best soccer player, and my teammates knew it. However, I showed up to every practice, and I played at least a few minutes of every game. By showing up, I supported the team, and the guys saw that and respected me for it. They saw that I was a little bit weird, but they looked past it because we shared a common bond on the field.

Third, some of the games were actually fun. The most memorable game I played was a game that turned into a mud bath. We were traveling to an away game when it began to rain heavily on the way there. We changed, ran to the field, and were soaked before we got into our starting positions. As we ran up and down the field defending our goal and passing the slippery ball between us; our cleats dug into the soft ground and created a muddy turf we began to slip and slide in. The mud-covered grass presented a challenge, but it was the most fun I'd had all season. I don't remember who won that game, but by the end, we were splattered with mud head to toe.

The most influential, positive outcome from being on the soccer team was the start of a friendship with Alyssa that carried me through my last two years of high school. Alyssa played on the girls' soccer team. We met on the field as we practiced together and often traveled to games together.

Alyssa was my rock and my solace. She understood me and accepted me without question. I felt comfortable around her in a way that I never had with anyone else before. I could truly be myself around her. When we were together, the world was kind again; I had no fear. The place we created was a utopian oasis where laughter, comfort, ease, and excitement prevailed. She brought out the very best in me. She taught me not to care what others thought, but to enjoy the life we were living with the talents we were given. She helped me discover and develop those talents and did so with a whole lot of fun.

One of the unique interests we shared was our love for *I Love Lucy*. Actually, we were obsessed with the show, quoted it often, and spent many an afternoon huddled around the TV watching Lucy and Ethel getting up to no good while snacking on salt-and-vinegar chips and Code Red Mountain Dew.

There was one episode where Lucy tries an at-home scalp treatment on Ricky because he's afraid he's going bald. She adds several ingredients to Ricky's hair and makes a mess out of the scene to make it comical.

So, naturally, Alyssa and I took it upon ourselves to recreate that scene in her kitchen. I sat down in a chair and draped a towel over myself. She set out the ingredients in a methodical order, and we were ready to go. She started by pouring vinegar on my hair and then massaged it in with some vegetable oil (I had greasy hair for days afterward). She then took an egg and cracked it over my head and made sure to get all of it all over me. Next, she took a cup of flour and powdered my hair. The laughter was worth the mess.

This wouldn't be the only time we wasted eggs in one of our bright ideas. I remember one day we decided to have an egg toss to see how far we could toss an egg to one another without it breaking. My mother became very annoyed when she found out we had used a dozen eggs as we kept trying to break our distance record.

After one Halloween, she convinced me to go to school with a few blacked-out teeth from the leftover putty we had from our costumes. We walked into our home room with our rotten, broken-looking teeth and took our seats; we couldn't stop snickering. We became a huge disruption, which won us a spot in detention that day.

Both Alyssa and her dad were great musicians who sang and played piano. He worked at the local university as the director of the theater department, and Alyssa learned to play piano as a hobby. The first time I walked into her house, I immediately saw a polished oak grand piano toward the back of the living room, perfectly placed on a small elevated platform. I'd never seen such a piano in someone's living room before. I let out an audible, "Wow!" and walked right over to it. I slid my hand across the lid, feeling the smoothness of this incredible instrument as I pressed on a few keys. What a beautiful sound that reverberated in the living room of my friend's house.

It was a tradition in their house to have music nights when a few of their musician friends came over and played into the night. These evenings consisted of Alyssa's dad on the piano, one of their friends on the violin, and another friend playing the cello. They played a mix of hymns with Broadway ballads sprinkled in between. And sometimes we sang along to the accompaniment they made. I always sat there in pure amazement as the orchestral sound filled the room. And I felt as if it penetrated deep into my soul, giving me a feeling of ecstasy. I couldn't help but close my eyes and smile as the melodies carried my heart.

Then I heard Alyssa calling my name to come up and sing with her. I timidly replied, "No, no. I can't. And I don't even know what we would sing."

Alyssa, the problem-solver, said, "Oh, it's OK. We'll find something. Actually, we should sing 'Ten Minutes Ago' from the live-action *Cinderella*."

The live-action Cinderella? *As in the one with the prince I had a crush on?* I thought

I walked up to the piano, where Alyssa met me, and her dad was seated flipping through the pages of the *Cinderella* songbook. I couldn't believe they actually had the real songbook.

Alyssa's dad started the introduction, and there was no turning back now. Alyssa and I fumbled our way through the duet, sharing tiny snickers and laughs as we sang like no one was listening. Our little duet ignited a fire within me.

Chapter Five

My junior year (and my first year) at the new school, I joined the choir. And it was cool because I noticed that most of the guys on the soccer team also were in the choir. There wasn't this big division between sports and music. This was a place where people could be artsy and sporty. I never married the two because one always seemed more masculine than the other. The joining of the two built a wonderful comradery between my peers and me as we ran around a soccer field chasing a ball and then joined together in song in the classroom. And even though choir seemed like a girly activity to join, my parents supported the decision.

Not long after joining the choir, I started voice lessons with the choir director. I loved them. It was there that I learned I had a gift for music. After that discovery, I directed my attention toward improving my voice during my last two years of high school.

I had voice lessons for one hour every week, and I looked forward to it. The teacher took great time getting to know my voice by engaging in certain exercises and choosing songs that fit my voice. He never tried to change my voice to sound like something different like many voice teachers do; rather, he gave me techniques to use to strengthen and improve the overall quality.

I remember vividly when he helped me find my vibrato. Before, I sang with a forced and tense sound, mostly due to nerves. But he taught me how to relax my legs, arms, chest, neck and jaw in order to allow my voice to carry its natural sound. He told me to sing and hold a note as I gently pressed my hands against my jaw and moved it ever so slightly. He told me to hold out the note and relax as much as possible until the vibrato came naturally and not forced. I closed my eyes, massaged my jaw on the note, and suddenly heard an even vibrato emerge. I immediately opened my eyes in surprise and saw my director standing in front of me with an expression of joy and excitement saying, "That's it! Now do it again!"

I will never forget that groundbreaking moment for me. My voice was still growing and maturing, so we didn't push the limits too hard, but I learned many more fundamental techniques that I carried with my throughout high school and on to college. Music gave me something to be joyous about. I remember thinking that I could finally actually do something, something that I could be good at.

Every year, the school hosted a fall concert. One of the songs we performed that night was a medley from *Les Misérables*. Included in the medley was the iconic "Bring Him Home" piece. The choir director asked if I would like to take the solo part of this song. I apprehensively agreed. Who was the "him" I was singing about anyway? Would people find it weird that I was singing about whomever this "him" was? Despite my questions, I worked diligently on my part. As I sang during practice, my peers gave surprised looks at what they heard. I finished and faded into the background of the choir. They expressed their surprise and congratulated me on a job well done.

Singing gave me a thrill and ignited a passion I couldn't tame. I loved being on stage. I adored singing, and people seemed to enjoy hearing me sing. I'd never in my life had so much positive affirmation from other people. I wasn't used to this level of acceptance. I felt like I'd finally found a way to both charm the masses and discover a defense strategy to deflect all the hateful comments hurled toward me over the past several years.

It was within my voice where I found a place to hide, a place to unload all of my sadness, depression, anger, and fear. Music became a stronghold I clung to with dear life as I began to express myself through singing. I discovered a safe place in music. When I was on stage, no one made fun of me. For once, they were quiet and listened intently.

At the end of one of my voice lessons, I thanked my teacher for his time and walked out of the front doors of the school where my mom was waiting to pick me up. As I walked over to the car, I thought, *I love singing. Could I really be this happy?*

In the spring of my junior year of the high school, I tried out for the school play, which was directed by Alyssa's dad, Dr. Maxwell. That year they were doing *The Importance of Being Earnest*. I tried out for the part of Jack Worthing. I received the lines for my part and rehearsed them over and over again in my room until I knew them by heart. Acting excited me. There was something about stepping into another person's life that intrigued me.

Auditions were held at the school and took place after classes. Several people showed up, including a few guys on the soccer team and Alyssa. As I got up to act out my scene, I felt nervous because I wanted this part badly, but I also felt a calming presence within the character I portrayed. At that moment, I was no longer Jordan but Jack. And he wasn't nervous in that scene. He was confident while trying to woo the girl he liked.

After the auditions ended, we were told that parts would be assigned in the next few days. Waiting for the parts to be posted felt like an eternity. I was up against two other guys for the part of Jack, but I knew I wanted it more than they did. I spent the next few days hoping and praying I'd see my name after Jack Worthing's.

At last, the day came. I went into school that morning eager to see the cast list. I ran up to the board and scanned the top of the page until I found the character list.

The Importance of Being Earnest

Cast List

Jack Worthing - - - - - - - - Jordan Roberts

I let out a big, "Oh my gosh! I made it!"

Alyssa was cast as Lady Bracknell. We shared a big hug, jumping up and down as we let out a few screams of excitement. I went home that day and shared with my parents the great news. They congratulated me on a job well done. My heavy involvement in the arts at school didn't win me a butch man card, but my parents were supportive of the Christian environment surrounding the arts scene.

Receiving my first full script gave me goose bumps. I held onto it with pride, not only because acting was special but also because the part was something I'd worked for and earned.

That first night, I opened the script to the first page and started to read from cover to cover. Then I took a highlighter and highlighted my lines throughout the work. I made little notes in the margins about different moods the character I was playing was having and how I thought he felt. I enjoyed studying the character, learning about him, and getting to know him through his responses and interactions with others in the script.

I looked forward to our first day of rehearsal. We went around the room and gave three adjectives for how we would describe our characters. When it came to my turn, I said that Jack was respectable, whimsical, and humorous.

We had rehearsals twice a week in the beginning and then more frequently closer to the performance. Play practice was the highlight of my week. I enjoyed acting with my peers and Dr. Maxwell was so kind and patient in the way that he instructed us. He just didn't tell us to do something differently—he showed us what he wanted. I gleaned as much from him as I could, and my acting improved from just delivering the lines to becoming a part of the character.

We had two dress rehearsals before our three-show run. At the dress rehearsal, we ran through the whole performance without stopping. We put on our clothing from wardrobe, and then we sat for makeup completed by a few students who wanted to be a part of the play but not act.

Putting on the makeup was another part of the play that made me feel whole. When I put on Jack's clothing and painted my face, I felt like I left Jordan behind and became this character that I made up in this story. It provided me an escape from reality, and I thrived in this imaginary oasis.

I remember driving home one night after a dress rehearsal in full makeup. Most of the other cast members removed theirs before they left, but I kept mine because I felt like it gave me a sort of power I didn't have as Jordan. When I got home, I walked into the house and into the bathroom. I stared at myself in the mirror for a bit and then took a cloth and removed the life-giving character.

When I entered my senior year of high school I was seventeen years old and my parents did something I never thought they would ever do. They allowed me to have a computer in my own room. I could tell my mom wasn't happy about this decision as she frequently stated that there wasn't a need to have a computer in my room. A computer behind closed doors invited too much temptation, she said. But my dad was open to the idea of allowing me to have a bit more freedom and independence. So I got a refurbished computer and put it in my room. Of course, I said I would use it mostly for school and listening to music. And I did do those things, as well as others.

Since looking up male Abercrombie & Fitch models online, my desire to search more images never went away. In fact, the urge became stronger. Now that I had my own computer in my room, my interest in searching models grew ever so strongly.

Late at night after everyone had gone to bed, I would climb out of my bed and slip into my desk chair. I'd press the power button on my computer and anxiously wait for it to load the home screen. I'd connect to the internet (yes, this was a time before high-speed internet) and open up Google images. In the search bar, I'd type things like "Male Model" or "Male Underwear Model." As the images of half-naked men filled the screen, I became overwhelmed by all of the choices of photos I had before me. I'd slowly click through each image until I found a guy I thought was particularly attractive, find his name, and start searching that model, specifically.

I made this almost a nightly routine. But an overwhelming sense of shame filled my heart and mind. I felt so badly for the sin I'd committed and prayed fervently for God to forgive me. I'd moan in repentance and hit myself angrily for allowing myself to engage in such unnatural and disgusting behavior.

This cycle of sinning and repenting lasted through the next several months until I felt so badly that I decided it was time to confess my sin to my parents.

One evening, my dad was sitting on the couch doing some work, and I was practicing piano a few feet away from the couch. As I played through some of the songs I'd been practicing, my mind raced with whether I should tell my dad what I'd been doing on the computer. Hiding it kept gnawing away at me, but I also didn't want to have that awkward conversation, and I certainly didn't want to voice my same-sex attraction. However, I resolved to just rip the Band-Aid off; I would say I was looking at straight porn to hopefully soften the blow. When I finished my song, I took my hands off of the keys and turned around in a very purposeful way to face my dad and said, "Okay, I need to confess something."

He looked up from what he was doing and said, "Okay, tell me anything."

I took a deep breath. "I have been struggling with looking at ungodly content on the internet. And I would like some help to stop."

My dad looked at me with kind eyes and said in a soft tone, "Sin is natural, son, and none of us are perfect. I'm so glad you told me."

I felt a sigh of relief and a sense of victory that I'd come clean and was ready to press on with full force ahead. We decided to keep the computer in my room for my convenience of doing homework, but downloaded a program called Covenant Eyes. This program tracked all websites and content viewed. Any suspicious content was sent to my dad as he was my accountability partner. In theory, this was an excellent program to keep one accountable for what is viewed on the internet, but it was only a matter of time before loopholes were found.

Chapter Six

aving a computer behind closed doors came with both responsibility and freedom. I was free to explore, but that came with a moral battle decide between right and wrong—a fight I often lost. The program that was installed on my computer was meant to be a barrier, which helped in the beginning. Then, I discovered that I could log onto the neighbor's Wi-Fi, bypassing the program's detection. The program was linked to our Wi-Fi and didn't track content from another router. This hack allowed me to continue my internet searches that went deep into the night. The images sent a tingle down my spine; *I wonder what it's like in real life?* I thought to myself. For the time being, the image was kept to my imagination.

For me, high school was a time of discovery. I not only found music but also found that I enjoyed public speaking and had a knack for Spanish.

I found an enjoyment for speech as I sat in my first speech class in eleventh grade. I liked public speaking because it gave me control of the situation. While I had no control over how people treated me outside, I took control and demanded attention when I was in front of the class. People listened. Something changed within me when I stepped into the spotlight. My voice became more confident, I moved with purpose, and I demanded the attention of my audience with my theatrical presence.

The teacher, who also happened to be Alyssa's mom, helped me develop my public speaking skills and saw in me potential I didn't know I had. I owe learning the fundamentals of public speaking to her, and I thank her for investing in me as I developed an enjoyment for public speaking. My favorite speech I gave was storytelling. I memorized a story called "You Are Special" by Max Lucado. It is a story about a little wooden boy who's different. He grows up in a society where it is customary for all of the wooden people to give each other stars and dots. Stars are like compliments and dots were given to show dissatisfaction. As in life, there were some people who walked around with many, many stars and few or no dots. And others who had nothing but dots and very little stars.

The main character had very little stars because he wasn't like the other kids growing up. He couldn't run as fast, jump as high, play sports as well, or sing as high as the other kids. Every time he tried to do something to prove his worth, he failed. And the kids laughed at him while sticking dots on him.

Until one day, he met someone. This someone was a carpenter who worked in a shop on top of a hill that overlooked the city. The little boy found this place to be comforting and inviting. The carpenter was very kind and greeted the boy with a warm smile. And this started a friendship where the little boy frequented the shop because it was a safe place for him. Eventually, the carpenter told the boy that it didn't matter what other people thought of him because they were just opinions from people who had no right to cast judgment on another. In fact, they had their own issues too. The carpenter told this little boy that the only opinion that mattered was the carpenter's. And this was because the carpenter made this little boy exactly the way he was supposed to be. And he was very, very special.

This story obviously resonated deep within me because I was that little boy. I connected with this story, and because of that, I was able to tell it with conviction and drama. I told this story with tears in my eyes, and my classmates listened intently. I looked at my teacher, who had a smile of approval on her face. She helped me find that story. And believe it.

For Alyssa's birthday that year, she wanted to go to New York City, which was a two-hour drive from where we lived. She invited me to celebrate with her and her parents. I'd never been to the Big Apple before, so I asked my parents if I could go celebrate with Alyssa, and they agreed. They knew Alyssa well and approved the majority of our requests. When we arrived, I was awestruck by the rhythm of the city. There were so many beautiful skyscrapers that it lived up to the name "a concrete jungle." The avenues were bumper to bumper with traffic, and the sounds of construction and car horns filled the air. Tourists from all over the world crowded the sidewalks, admiring the architecture. The diversity was eye-opening and exciting. We pushed our way through the crowds until we got to the theater district. My eyes widened at the sight of the marquee signs and flashing lights of all the Broadway shows currently playing. We went straight to the box office of the Neil Simon Theatre where the show *Hairspray* was playing. I'd never heard of the show before and was just along for the ride. We put our names in a lottery, which gave us a chance to win tickets at a discounted price. As luck would have it, we won four tickets for the 2:00 p.m. show. We couldn't believe it, and I had no idea what I was about to experience.

Hairspray was unforgettable. We arrived at the theater thirty minutes before the show started. We took our seats in the very front row, just feet from the stage; we could reach out and touch it if we'd wanted to. This perspective gave us an up-close look at the actors as they frequently came to the front of the stage. We could see their overly dramatic expressions and big movements that reached the audience all the way in the back of the theater. I saw the actors spit as a result of clear diction so that the words were understood with ease. I was mesmerized for the entire two and a half hours as the performers transported me into their world. The actors, the lights, the stage, the setting, the costumes, the makeup were so good that I couldn't help but stare in amazement as the show communicated something magical to my soul. For those enchanted hours, I was no longer in NYC, but I was in the streets of Baltimore living the story they were telling through dance and music.

The show-stopping moment for me was when Darlene Love sang "I Know Where I've Been." I remember like it was yesterday when she belted out the last few bars of the ballad. My jaw quite literally dropped open as I listened to a voice unlike any other I'd heard before. I didn't want the show to end, and as we walked out of the theater, I remained speechless. The icing on the cake was being able to meet the actors at the stage door as they left the theater. They signed our *Playbills* and even snapped a few photos with us. What a thrill it was to experience the magic of theater.

That day I felt the power of music. Music changed me. It ignited something within me that further intrigued my passion for the arts. This experience awakened my soul as I discovered the life-changing world of musical theater.

The other discovery I'd mentioned was finding a niche for Spanish. My Spanish teacher in high school was born in the United States but spent a large part of her adult life in Costa Rica. Her multicultural background, fluency in Spanish, and otherwise exciting life fascinated me. I asked her many questions about what it was like living in Costa Rica and how she'd learned Spanish fluently. She told me that the best way to learn was to fully immerse yourself in the culture and the language. She surrounded herself with Spanish-speaking people only. She also told me that she asked a lot of questions of people, even if she knew the answer. For example, even if she knew where the grocery store was, she would ask someone on the street to give her directions to the grocery store. This way she heard how they described it so she could learn the right sentence structure and word usage.

While in school, I met a lovely family from Venezuela who lived a few doors down from me. Arriving in the United States, they knew very little English but worked diligently to learn the language. This family had two boys who also attended the school I attended. The oldest was two years older than me, and the youngest was two years younger than me. Despite the small age gap, we enjoyed hanging out together.

I spent a lot of time with this family, and they often invited me into their home, sharing with me their culture, language, and food. I enjoyed learning something different from that which I knew. I was fascinated by their culture, and the food they prepared was delectable. One night, they invited me over for dinner, and I eagerly accepted. They'd prepared a traditional Venezuelan chicken dish with potatoes and other vegetables. As we sat down at the table, I could barely wait to taste all the wonderful flavors from this exotic kitchen. But before we filled our plates, we bowed our heads as the father said a prayer in Spanish. I remember hearing the wife interrupt her husband's prayer, whispering, "Mas lento," which means "slower." She knew I was trying to learn Spanish and reminded the family often to speak slowly and clearly.

As a result of spending time with them, I picked up on Spanish fairly quickly. I bought Spanish textbooks to help with the grammar, verbs, and vocabulary. I completed several chapter lessons at a time. I was eager to keep learning. I made flash cards with Spanish words on them to test my knowledge. I then put sticky notes all over the house, naming things such as the refrigerator, microwave, table, chairs, windows, blinds. You name it, it had a sticky note on it with the Spanish word for whatever it was. When you opened up the silverware drawer, you better believe that each section was labeled with the Spanish word for *spoon, knife,* and *fork.* My new friends checked over my work and corrected the errors I made.

Toward the end of my senior year of high school, my Spanish teacher asked me what my thoughts were for after graduation. I told her that I wasn't sure. I knew that I enjoyed music but thought that I would keep it as a hobby as I found a more sustainable job. I also thought about going into nursing. While I had a passion for the arts and language, science and medicine also intrigued me. My fascination with the human body came at an early age. I remember one day going to the library at the college my dad attended and asking to see an anatomy-and-physiology book. The librarian gave me a quizzical look and asked why I wanted to see such a volume. I'm sure she thought I was after the explicit pictures, but that wasn't the case. I simply wanted to learn.

She typed a few things into the computer and wrote down a library number on a small card and slid it across the desk to me. I took the key, found the section where the book was, and browsed the titles until I found the exact number on the card. I pulled out the book, found a comfy spot to sit, and started skimming the pages. I was fascinated by how detailed all of the pictures were. Everything was labeled. I came across the human brain and felt overwhelmed by how intricate it all was. But that didn't discourage me. I spent the next several minutes sifting through the pages and reading the side notes, just barely comprehending the words I read but knowing I wanted to learn more. And perhaps one day I would.

After patiently listening to me talk about these options, my Spanish teacher offered another option. She told me about an opportunity to study abroad in Argentina for one year. During the year, I would get college credit and be enrolled in a bilingual program where I would take Bible and Spanish classes during the first semester before transitioning into taking Bible classes in Spanish. My ears perked up hearing this. When

I arrived home that day, I researched the program and was interested. I presented this opportunity to my parents for approval. While it wasn't their first choice to send their youngest child five thousand miles away for college, they agreed to let me go. I filled out an application, and to my surprise, I was accepted into the program.

One of the hardest parts about leaving was saying goodbye to Alyssa. I remember we went to Starbucks—a place we often visited—to chat and share one last latte before we said our goodbyes. She was always supportive of me. I knew I would be back, but life changes so much in twelve months. This era we had created was about to end, and we both knew it. As I got in my car, backed out of my parking space, and pulled out of the lot, I could see Alyssa in my rearview mirror standing next to her car and waving at me as I drove away.

Chapter Seven

My trip to Argentina started by packing up the car at our house in Pennsylvania and driving two hours to JFK airport. My parents parked the car and escorted my two large suitcases, one carry-on, one personal item, and me to the ticket counter. When the ticket agent placed my bags on the scale, I held my breath and crossed my fingers that I didn't go over the weight limit. When a big "50" popped up on the screen, I let out a sigh of relief and unclenched my butt cheeks.

After I checked in and sent my bags down that mysterious conveyer belt, my parents told me how proud they were of me and gave me a big hug. This was the first time that I would be leaving home and not returning for a year. I hated goodbyes and didn't particularly enjoy being out of my comfort zone. I'd thought about this moment many times when I'd first started preparing to leave. And I wasn't looking forward to it. While my parents and I had our differences, they were still family. They were home. They were familiar, and I was getting ready to step into a completely unfamiliar world. I held back tears as the warm embrace of my parents' hug lingered. But I knew I had to let go.

I made my way through security, found my gate and patiently waited for boarding to begin. I was excited and nervous for what was ahead.

After an eleven-hour flight, we finally touched down in Buenos Aires. We arrived at our gate, and as soon as the seat belt sign was turned off, the sound of unclicking reverberated through the cabin as passengers jumped from their seats to gather their belongings and exit the aircraft.

The customs line was long, which is no surprise as we were not the only 777 aircraft carrying over three hundred people, all with the same idea of visiting Argentina or returning home. I had butterflies in my stomach as I stood in line waiting to get my passport stamped. I kept thinking, *What if they don't let me through? Or what if they ask me a question I don't know the answer to? Do they speak English or will I have to rely on my broken Spanish?* As I inched closer to the counter, I rehearsed over in my mind, *Hola, estoy aquí para turismo.* I was instructed by the college to ask for a tourist visa, which granted ninety days. And the visa would be renewed at the ninety days. This was the easiest way to get a visa.

It was finally my turn to step up to the agent. They looked at me with a routine smile and asked, "Hola, prefieres Inglés or Español?" (Hello, do you prefer English or Spanish?)

Relieved, I replied, "Hello, English, please," and handed her my passport.

In a thick Spanish accent, she asked, "What is your purpose for visiting Argentina?"

"Tourism," I replied.

She put my passport through a scanner and held it up as she looked at the passport photo, then at me, back to the photo, and then me one last time. I gave an awkward smile as she studied my face against the photo presented.

She flipped through the empty pages of my passport as I shifted my weight, switching my heavy bag from one shoulder to the other. The agent took out her stamp, placed it on the ink pad and stamped my passport with a ninety-day visa.

She handed my passport back to me as she said, "Welcome to Argentina."

The college was situated on several acres of farmland. The entrance was secured by a locked gate and a guard who monitored those who entered and exited. As the marked van pulled up to the gate, we were waved through. We drove down a single-lane gravel road until we pulled in to the campus. I looked around at what would be my new home for the next year.

I got out and did a complete 360-degree view. To my left was the dining hall, where I noticed people sitting inside at tables talking to each other and passing around a small brown cup-looking thing with a metal straw coming out of it. I later found out that they were drinking something called *mate* (mah-tay), a traditional Argentine tea.

In front of me was a courtyard area with luscious shrubbery, a few towering palm trees, and flowers sprinkled throughout. To my right, I saw several buildings of all different sizes. They were placed around a large field of grass with a dirt path to each building along the entire length of the field. These buildings consisted of classrooms, offices, and dormitories. There were also tennis, volleyball, and basketball courts, and a soccer field that would be used on a daily basis.

Tucked a little farther back in the field, I noticed several small, bungalows. This is where the faculty and staff stayed. Housing was provided for those who worked at the college.

As I looked around, I noticed the sounds of farm animals, mostly the deep, bellowed moos from cows, that traveled through the distance. I learned that the college had a farm complete with massive gardens where all of the produce was grown that we would eat. In addition, the animals were raised for meat used to feed the students.

When the bags were unloaded, I was shown to my dormitory, which was a three-story building facing directly on the other side of the field. I took my bags and walked down the dusty path until I made it to the building entrance. I was on the top floor, and there were no elevators. So I had no choice but to drag my fifty-pound suitcases up three flights of stairs. Watching a 120-pound scrawny kid try to navigate his way up those stairs must have been a spectacle to see. But I got them all up and wheeled them to where I would be staying.

When I walked into my room, there were two sets of bunk beds on either wall and one bunk bed up against the wall opposite of the door. Between the two sets of bunk beds on the side walls were small cubbies assigned to each occupant. These provided a small place to store clothes and any other belongings. Not much for organization, but it did encourage a minimalist lifestyle. Not to mention, most of the students didn't have a lot to their names anyway.

One large bathroom was located at the end of the hallway on each floor. There was a row of five sinks upon entering the bathroom. To the left were six stalls and six urinals each on the opposite side of each other. To the right were six showers, three on each side. As I scanned the bathroom, I noticed that there were no shower curtains. I was both confused and mortified. *How will I ever be able to take a shower with my naked body on display in front of everyone?* I thought. I turned around and headed back to my room.

I had six roommates during my first semester. One guy was a former bilingual program student from Florida who chose to stay at the college for additional learning. There was a guy from Guatemala, one from Peru, Bolivia, Panama, and the Dominican Republic. To my delight, we all got along well.

Acclimating to life in South America wasn't easy, but I was determined to use this time to enhance my relationship with God. Also, I missed my family, and I suffered a great deal from something I'd never experienced before—homesickness. I'd never missed the familiar as much I did in those beginning days (and weeks) of living in this entirely new environment so far away from my family.

When I felt extremely sad, I held on to things that reminded me of home. My mom packed me a set of towels, and I remember looking at and clinging onto the towels because it made me feel closer to home. My mom also bought me an iPod before I left so that I wouldn't have to carry all my CDs with me. I loved the gift because it was from my mom, and it was thoughtful. I downloaded all of the albums I had and played them often as they, too, helped me feel closer to home.

Music is the language of emotion. It connects us to our feelings and helps us express ourselves when words fail. When I was feeling down, I listened to the original cast recording of the musical *The Secret Garden*. I enjoyed this musical because it told a story of growth and hope in the midst of sadness. One of the main characters dies during childbirth. But she's kept alive through a garden that was renewed after years of neglect.

The themes of hope and comfort come through the fact that while a loved one may not be physically present, they are still with us, whether that be in spirit or through something tangible that's meaningful to that individual.

The story allowed me to escape my reality, and for those moments, I felt OK. The angelic sounds comforted my weary soul. Music is a solace that endorses strength and comfort when we're surrounded with unsettling and fearful emotions. Living in Argentina was very uncomfortable for me. Not because of the culture, language or people, but because of the conditions I was living in. I had one question for myself, *What in the world did I sign up for?*

Chapter Eight

The college was split into two programs. There was the bilingual program, which offered students who speak English the opportunity to study Spanish and earn a Bible certificate. The second program offered a Bible degree to those students who already spoke Spanish. It would be like going to a Christian college in the States.

In the bilingual program, the first semester included rigorous Spanish courses and Bible classes taught in English. At the start of the second semester, everyone in the bilingual program enrolled in the college where everything was taught in Spanish. By this time, it was expected that those in the bilingual program would be able to adequately communicate, understand, speak, read and write in Spanish on a college level. And most us of came into the program with foundational Spanish-speaking skills.

At orientation, all students were given a weekly itinerary that mapped out each day's activities. The college established this daily schedule that had to be followed with few to no exceptions. It reminded me of a camp schedule where every hour was filled with an activity. College was supposed to be a place where freedom was gained, not lost. But that wasn't the motto here. The college taught that having structure in your daily life reflected the strength and maturity of your spiritual life.

My daily schedule looked something like this:

7:00 breakfast

8:00 devotional

8:20–10:00 class

10:00–10:30 break

10:30–12:00 class

12:00–13:00 lunch

13:00–15:00 work

15:00–17:00 sport

17:00–18:00 dinner

18:00–19:00 study

20:00–22:00 quiet time

22:00 lights out

On Tuesday, Wednesday, and Friday, we had chapel service.

At that time, we were also handed a rule book. I knew that the college was conservative, but what I read came as a bit of a shock. The rules were not lenient, and I felt like I needed to carry around a flash card to remember them all. For example, the dress code was very strict. For men, business casual was to be worn at all times during class hours. During chapel, a tie must be worn; a suit must be worn while at church on Sundays. Men couldn't have their hair touching the ears or have facial hair and side burns must not go below the earlobe. They must be clean shaven on a daily basis, even when there was no hot water. For women, they must wear skirts or dresses in class and at church. Pants were permitted outside of class. And no one could leave campus without written permission during specific hours.

Several times a semester, the dean of men would call meetings where all the men had to be in attendance. At these meetings, he would talk about pornography and masturbation, preaching how it was the way of sinfulness and a work of the devil. *So that's why they took the shower curtains away*, I thought. They were adamant about fleeing from any sort of temptation that might influence someone toward sexual activity of any kind.

For the next several weeks, I woke up at 5:00 a.m. I would tiptoe into the shower as most of the guys were still sleeping. I would wash off quickly and tiptoe back to my room, where I got dressed in the dark before I made my way to the dining hall, where I would sit until breakfast at 7:00 a.m. I used this time to journal. My routine worked out for a couple of weeks until I became more comfortable with my surroundings.

One of the first times I walked into the shower room, I remember feeling a sense of relief when I saw that no one else was there. I set my shower basket on a ledge near the shower, hung up my towel, and turned on the water, being careful not to fully immerse myself until the water was somewhat hot. I washed my hair, scrubbed my face, and stood under the hot water as I relaxed under its constant pulse against my skin.

After a few moments, I noticed a guy walking into the room with a towel around his waist and a shower basket similar to mine. He placed his basket on a ledge near his shower and turned on the water. He was handsome. He was about my height of five ten. He had beautiful olive skin and a strong jawline. I tried to keep my eyes to myself but couldn't help but look over at him as he patiently waited for his water to warm. Then, he took off his towel and hung it up on the ledge. His beautiful physique was fully exposed before me. I felt myself stop breathing for a brief moment. I'd never seen a naked man in person before, and my heart beat with fascination. I knew I shouldn't look or even want to look, but I couldn't help but steal a few peeks, trying to be as inconspicuous as possible. I shook myself out of the trance I was in and scrubbed my body with soap as to make it seem like I was minding my own business. But I could still see him in my peripheral vision, and I made frequent glances in his direction. I thought to myself, *"Maybe this won't be so bad after all."*

There were a few other guys in my cohort that I made friends with, one of whom was Joseph. Joseph was the class clown and lived on a high energy level. He had a sweet personality and an infectious laugh. His aura was inviting, and everyone enjoyed being around him. There came a point in our program where we all started taking showers at the same time because our schedules matched up. And Joseph was good at making light of uncomfortable situations. He called this time together "Shower Hour." He loved to sing, among many other things, so we spent this time singing Disney songs or just harmonizing on random notes we sang. If other people were showering at the same time, sometimes they would join in if they knew the words or had good harmonizing skills. It turned out to be quite fun.

I began to enjoy showering because I knew it would include other men I could look at. And the real thing was just as good as the pictures I'd seen on my computer screen in my bedroom in high school. Deep down, I felt like l was sinning by looking at these guys and enjoying it. It was also a bit scary to realize that this inward struggle wasn't just a phase or just something in my imagination. I was attracted to these men. But what did that mean for my spirituality? Was I going to hell now? Over the next few months, these questions began to burn in my mind and stir up a lot of emotions in my heart.

There were about forty students in my cohort that year. I immediately hit it off with one of my classmates. Her name was Rachael. Before long, we had discovered a common interest in plays, musical theater, Shakespeare, poetry, and coffee. Every week, we set up a time and location to get together for a "coffee date." She taught me how to make a delicious drink with instant coffee (that's all we had). First, she placed the instant coffee in a mug. Then, she poured a little bit of hot water and sugar over the coffee grounds and stirred vigorously until the mixture frothed. She then added more water or milk to fill the mug. It was her own version of a latte fashioned from the resources we had. She made us this latte drink as we chatted about movies, poetry, and the latest books we had been reading. I treasured these times we shared.

One of my favorite parts of the week was going to the nearby town. At certain times during the week, we were able to leave the campus and walk or take a taxi into town. Before leaving, we had to request permission from a designated staff member, and it was up to them whether permission was granted. If he felt the reason for leaving wasn't good enough or was just having a bad day, then he could decline the request. Most often, requests were granted. We were then given a slip with the time we'd left and the time we had to be back, which was usually within three hours. We showed this permission to the guard at the gate and then again when we returned. If we returned outside the window, then we would get a demerit and win ourselves a meeting with the dean. A demerit usually consisted of doing an extra odd job around campus.

But going through all of that interrogation was worth the trips to town. Normally, a few of us from the cohort and sometimes other students from the college would walk into town, which was about a mile walk. It was a nice break to be on the other side of the walls of the college. Going to town felt liberating, and it was neat to see Argentina as the locals lived.

There was a restaurant called Rosies, which served the best Italian-inspired food I had there. The calzones were bigger than my face and cost less than a loaf of bread in the States. The workers there got to know us quite well as we frequently gorged ourselves on the rich cuisine served. There was another restaurant called Mango that served steak that cut like butter and melted in your mouth while releasing a burst of flavors with each bite.

Trips to town provided an escape from the otherwise stifling regime of daily living at the college. As time passed and we became more comfortable with our surroundings, a few classmates and I started to push the boundaries. We realized that we could easily leave without anyone noticing if the guard left his post or was busy giving his attention to something else. We snuck out a few times but always returned within a good time; we didn't want to push our luck too much.

But one afternoon, we decided to stay out a little past the time they required us to be back, which was by 6:00 p.m. There were four of us who walked to town and went to our favorite spot, Rosies. We shared a few calzones, a two-liter bottle of Coca-Cola, and some sides of French fries with chimichurri sauce. Argentina is also known for their Malbec and other wines, so we thought, *What would it hurt to have a little wine tasting?*

This was the first time I'd tasted wine. And my palette wasn't ready for a dry red wine such as a Malbec. I remember sipping it, and an overwhelming taste of alcohol swirled my mouth and burned down my throat. The full-bodied wine dried out my tongue as if I'd placed a few cotton balls in my mouth. With that, I pushed the glass away, refusing to drink more.

Noticing that the time was past 6:00 p.m., we decided to make our way back to the campus. While we knew it could be easy to leave, we didn't, however, realize that after hours, staff members patrolled the road nearing the campus gate. As we were walking and getting closer to campus, we noticed a familiar staff member riding a bike and approaching us. He knew we were students.

He barked a question at us. "Que hacen ustedes?" (What are you all doing?)

"Estamos regresando del pueblo." (We are returning from town.) I said with a hope for no other follow-up questions,

He asked with an accusatory tone, "Ya es tarde. Por qué están regresando a esta hora?" (It's late. Why are you guys returning so late?),

I replied, "Estabamos cenando y nos perdimos la noción del tiempo." (We were eating dinner and lost track of time.)

He escorted us back through the gate and said, "Ustedes deben pasar por la oficina para conversar por llegar tarde." (You guys need to stop by the office and talk about arriving late.)

I had a sick feeling in my stomach and knew that we could be in big trouble. But the four of us never stopped by the office, and to my surprise, no one came looking for us.

Part of being a student was working on campus. This work included cleaning, landscaping, working on the farm, laundry services, meal prep and kitchen services etc. which kept the cost of attendance low and helped build structure and responsibility in the lives of the students, which many benefited from.

My first job was cleaning the dormitories and bathrooms. If you don't know, in South America, the toilet paper cannot be flushed. Rather, there is a trash can beside each toilet for used items. Between dumping the trash cans, cleaning up body hair, and wiping up urine stains, I would say that I deserved a prize. I couldn't let myself become too miserable, though, so I had to find the silver lining. With this job, I could work alone, take my time, watch my progress, listen to soothing music, and be relieved I wasn't out in the field picking rocks or chopping the heads off chickens. There was much to be thankful for if I was willing to be thankful for it. That semester came to an end, and I wouldn't be cleaning toilets anymore.

My second job was cleaning the small elementary school that was on campus. There were four other people in my group and Paula, the supervisor. I didn't know much about the school's existence before I was assigned to clean it. The kids of the faculty and staff sent their kids here, and I believe it was also open to the public, so long as you met the standard of Christian living set forth by the code of conduct. It was, after all, a Christian school.

Cleaning the school was much better than cleaning bathrooms. There were five classrooms that we cleaned along with the halls and two bathrooms, one for the boys and the other for the girls. Included in the group were two girls, two boys, and me. We all got along great, and I enjoyed talking to them as we tag-teamed cleaning the classrooms. One person swept and mopped the floor while the other cleaned the chalkboard, wiped off the desks, and took out the trash. We would then alternate roles every other room.

We always completed our jobs in record time, which left some free time to do whatever we wanted. Most of the time, though, we hung out outside of the school and shared a basket of pan dulce purchased from the bodega on campus, which outsourced the delicious treats from the local bakery. Each week we took turns providing the assortment of sweets, including bread with dulce de leche or chocolate, strawberry or cream filling, or just plain sweet bread. My favorite was the bread with dulce de leche.

One of the primary focuses at the college was evangelism. As Christians, it was our duty to spread the good news of the gospel of Jesus whether people wanted to listen or not. We were instructed to commit verses to memory, and we were given Bible tracts to hand out to people we saw when we were out in town. In one of our Bible classes, we had a training day where we practiced evangelizing each other. We were given a list of possible questions: Where did God come from? Why do bad things happen? Why should I believe in Jesus? Where am I going to go when I die? We were given answers to all of these questions with Bible verses we memorized. The answers we were given included demonstrating faith and taking God's word as truth. We told people that they had to believe by faith or else they wouldn't go to heaven.

There were specific days scheduled when we would go out into the community and spread the news with our scripted knowledge. We would interrupt people on their walks or as they had a picnic in the park. "Would you like to hear about Jesus?" or "Do you know where you will spend eternity when you die?" we said as we approached them. Most people looked at us quizzically and respectfully declined. But we weren't to stop there. We would ask, "May I ask why you don't want to talk about it? Do you know that Jesus loves you?" If they still wouldn't engage in conversation, we recited a Bible verse, left a tract and moved on.

Approaching people like this always made me feel uncomfortable. Why did we have to do this? Essentially, we were smothering people with the Bible, and when they didn't engage, we relegated it to their sinfulness. It felt wrong, and embarrassing.

I tried my best to talk to the fewest people possible. When I could, I went off by myself and walked around. Sometimes, I gave a hello and engaged in small talk with some bystanders to make it look like I was trying to convert them. I wanted to be normal. I didn't want to give people a reason to judge me, much like when we'd pray as a family at a restaurant growing up.

At the end of the day, we gathered together and gave numbers of how many people accepted the gospel, or rather, accepted Jesus in their hearts to be saved. I'd hear numbers from people yelling enthusiastically, "Seven!" "Ten!" "Five!" "Twelve!" And I would say, "Two." The leader of the group would congratulate all the work and say, "So many souls added to the Book of Life and will now go to heaven!"

I thought, *How do we know they meant it, and we didn't just scare them into repeating a few words in the name of prayer? Who is going to follow up with them?* It felt like the motivation in this evangelism was numbers, which gave them more fervency to beat their last record. I didn't buy into this tactic, and I really didn't care. I had other things on my mind. Burdens that kept me up at night and fears that shook my turbulent heart.

Chapter Nine

While in Argentina, I further battled who I was inside. The questions that I asked myself standing under the water in the showers continued to press on my heart. I fell deeper into the Christian environment that reinforced this idea that I was an abomination in the eyes of God. This confusing feeling grew as I questioned God without receiving answers in return. It was a battle I fought on my own and the wounds went deep. I became withdrawn and depressed. I remember faking sickness so I wouldn't have to participate in the required activities built into our schedules, such as playing the sport that was assigned to us, participating in special game nights or going to work. I purposefully stopped drinking water in hopes of dehydrating myself. I lowered my caloric intake. I didn't engage in self-harm long-term, but I did it enough to use it as an outlet, which started a pattern of harmful coping mechanisms. To my delight, I did end up contracting strep throat, which gave me a week of reprieve, but it wasn't enough.

All the students at the college were assigned mentors so that we could be held accountable to stay true to the Word of God. I set up a meeting with my mentor and told him I needed to discuss something important with him. His parents were lifetime faculty members at the college and occupied a large house on the campus. One afternoon, my mentor invited me to their house so we could talk. The house didn't remind me of a humble Argentine house like the previously mentioned bungalows. Their place reminded me of a large farmhouse, complete with a wraparound porch. It was beautiful.

I met my mentor at the house, and he invited me to take a seat in one of the wicker chairs on the porch. He offered me a glass of water or tea, and I said water was fine. He brought out a full glass, set it on a small table next to my chair, and sat down. He asked me how things were going, and I told him that everything was going fine. But I continued by saying that there was something I was struggling with, but I wasn't quite sure how to express it. He waited patiently as I tried to find the words to say to describe what I'd been going through. Where did I even start?

My heart was pounding inside my chest, and I racked my brain for the best way to explain the feelings I had. I shifted in my chair, leaned forward and took a gulp of the water he had brought me. I set the glass back down and leaned back in my chair. I finally looked at him and said, "There's no easy way to say this, so I'm going to just come right out and say it, no pun intended."

He continued to look at me and wait for me to say whatever was on my mind.

"Uh, okay. Um... well I, uh, I... I have been struggling with same-sex attraction, and I need help."

He looked at me almost as if I'd admitted to him that I had a communicable disease.

He said, "Well, Jordan, we can get you the help that you need. And the next time you're having these ungodly thoughts, come talk to me instead of dwelling on them."

I nodded that I would.

He continued by telling me that I wasn't a homosexual; rather, I was dealing with an addiction. And I believed him. I wanted to be set free from the bondage I was in. He also told me that he felt it was necessary to discuss this matter with the dean of students. I had no more fight left in me, and I wanted to end the war. I thought that by confessing who I was would provide liberation from the lifelong conundrum I had going on inside me. And I was partially right. I did feel a bit freer, but something with his response didn't feel right.

On my walk back to my dorm, I replayed the events in my head, and I felt like I had done something wrong by telling him. I felt self-concious. It was like going to the doctor to reveal something embarrassing—you know you have to do it, but it doesn't help you feel better. After talking to him, he treated me like I was sick and the Bible was my medicine.

I thought that perhaps my discomfort was part of the healing process and would improve once I came totally clean with my parents. That same day, I mustered up the courage to call my parents on a Skype phone my friend let me borrow. I walked down to the common area, which had internet access. I found a secluded spot and sat myself down on the ground with my back resting against a wall. I logged on to the internet and dialed my parents' number. I took a deep breath and pressed the send button. I put the phone up to my ear and listened as the phone rang on the other end. After a few seconds, I heard my dad's voice.

"Hello?"

I closed my eyes tightly, bit my lips, and fought the urge to cry. Just hearing my dad's voice was enough to send me into an emotional breakdown. His voice was familiar and comforting. But I did my best to compose myself

"Hey, Dad, it's Jordan," I said in a broken voice.

"Jordan! It's great to hear your voice!" he replied

"Thanks," I said. "Yours, too."

"How've you been doing? We are eager to hear about how things are going there," he said enthusiastically.

"I have been OK," I said. "But I need to talk to you about something."

"Of course. Anything," he said in a more serious tone.

There was a long pause as I fought back tears, again.

"Is everything OK?" my dad said with more concern.

"I have been dealing with a lot through my life. And I feel like I'm struggling with same-sex attraction. And the content I searched on the internet I told you about wasn't women—it was men," I explained through bursts of tears.

"I love you so much, Jordan," my dad said without hesitation "And there is a way we can fight this. No sin is greater than God."

I held the phone up to my ear without saying anything. The only thing passing through the phone were gentle sobs I could no longer keep in. My dad comforted me and told me that everything would be OK.

I told my dad that I was scared that I wasn't saved, that God didn't love me. And I was even afraid to fall asleep because what if I didn't wake up? What happens then?

He interrupted me by saying, "The fact that you're so bothered by this shows me that you're saved. If you weren't, you wouldn't be so worried."

His words were comforting.

My dad told me to do what they recommended about my same-sex attraction and finish out the program. He then told me that when I got home, I could start biblical counseling. He told me that he would share this news with my mom and that they would be praying for me. And he reiterated his thankfulness for me taking the right steps.

On that note, we ended our conversation and hung up.

I got myself up, wiped my tears with my shirt, and walked back to my dorm room.

A few days later, my mentor approached me and told me that he had spoken with the dean, and he wanted to have a meeting. We planned a meeting for that afternoon. I became very nervous at the thought of speaking with the dean of students about my sexual sins. After all, this was the man who held all of those men's meetings condemning any sort of sexual transgressions both of physical or perceptual nature. *What will he say about me?* I thought. But my secret was already out in the open, so I had to confess, for the third time.

I walked from the dining hall, through the courtyard, and into one of the administrative buildings. I could feel my heart racing and my thoughts were scattered. I was just confused, but I knew I wanted to do what was right in the eyes of my parents and those who were placed in leadership over me. While I felt embarrassed, confession of sin was necessary to heal, according to the Bible.

I met my mentor there, and we walked to the dean's office. When we arrived at his door, he motioned us to come in and take a seat. It looked like a typical office. It was well-lit where the sun shone through a single window, and a fluorescent light was overhead. He had a wood desk with an ancient HP computer monitor and a tower beside it. He had a few family pictures neatly placed across his desk along with some documents that looked to be for the school. There were two wooden chairs directly in front of the desk where my mentor and I took seats.

The dean was a stern man who appeared to be all about business and left little room for levity. He was typically seen wearing a suit unless working outside. He was an older man, about five eleven, completely bald, and he wore glasses with thin, metal frames. Having lived and worked on the farm for most of his life, he had the build of a farmer. His demeanor was serious; he was an authoritarian.

He began the conversation. "Bueno, empezamos?" (Okay, shall we begin?)

The dean didn't speak English, so this conversation would be held in Spanish. I was growing in my Spanish, but still not fluent. So, adequately expressing my deep emotional issues presented a challenge, but they wanted to hear from me specifically. And my mentor helped out with specific word usage where he could.

"Bienvenidos, buenas tardes. Entiendo que tienes algo de que hablar. No?" (Welcome, good afternoon. I understand that you have something to talk about, right?)

I nodded and replied, "Buenas tardes, gracias por recibirme. Si, tengo unas luchas muy profundas de las que me gustaria hablar." (Good afternoon, thanks for having me. Yes, I have a few deep issues that I would like to talk about.)

As I sat uncomfortably in the chair, I took a deep breath and began to articulate my thoughts and feelings. As I spoke, I squeezed my hands together in a rhythmic motion as if I were washing them. It was a nervous tick. While the conversation was held in Spanish, it will be presented in English for ease of reading.

"I have been struggling with a specific sin for a long time." I said.

I continued, "I feel like I have an attraction toward men as if I were a homosexual."

The stern man across from me tilted is head forward and looked at me over his glasses without blinking an eye. And then he asked me a couple of follow-up questions.

First, he asked, "When do you have the urges to look at men?"

I explained to him, "Well, the majority of the time. It's not a case of when because it's all the time. When I'm walking down the street and I see a handsome guy, I look at him and think about him. It's not always in a sexual way, but I notice him. I don't do this with women. I don't look at them, and I don't notice them like I do men."

He then asked me his second question that took me by surprise.

"Sometimes men who think they are homosexuals have a micropenis." He held up a pencil and measured with his finger what that would be like as he spoke.

I gave a dubious look. *Is he kidding with this question?* I thought and said, "No, that's not my problem."

He nodded and explained to me that he had dealt with the problem I was having many times with other men and that he could help me. He told me that the men he had helped in the past are now married to women, have families, and live happily ever after. He also told me that to help get rid of this sinful desire and to teach me how to be a man, he would switch my job to start working on the farm. He said that by doing this manual labor, it would rewire my thinking and help me identify more as a man by reinforcing a man's work. I didn't love this idea of doing so much manual labor, but I was willing to put in the work to be another success story.

He said, "Then, Jordan, we will work together in the field at the farm and disinfect your soul. We will serve the Lord, do what is right, and He will bless us."

He got up from his chair, shook my hand and walked us out.

Working on the farm was tough. I dug holes and ditches. I picked out rocks from the field, planted vegetables, and harvested others that were ripe. I learned quite a bit about planting. And I enjoyed talking with some of the other guys as they helped improve my Spanish, especially as we discussed things like gardening, different types of vegetables, tools for harvesting, and many other things that I'd never done before.

I know that I was supposed to be doing this work to help get rid of my evil, homosexual thoughts, but how could I not get a little excited when I saw some of these sweaty guys flexing their muscles as they worked hard under the Argentine sun? For me, the work was worth the view, especially when they removed their shirts and wiped the sweat from their brows with their forearms.

I was brainwashed to think that I had a parasite growing in me, sucking the life out of me. I was told that I would never go to heaven unless I forsook my sin by crucifying this pathogen that was destroying me. And healing could be done with a little bit of prayer and some hard work.

Even with all of this extra labor, nothing changed. The battle continued. But because my allegiance to the Lord and obedience to His Word was the way to salvation, I wanted to remain faithful; however, how could I deny who I was? How could I strip myself of my very person? Not only was the arduous fight growing harder, but also, I was being forced to do things that I didn't want to do, but was willing to put up with. I wasn't excelling because I wasn't happy, and I wasn't where I belonged. They were trying to hammer a puzzle piece into the wrong place. But I tried to fit the best I could because I wanted to do what was right. I didn't want to disappoint anyone, and I wanted to live my most holy life, so that I could one day achieve the prize—heaven.

While I'd taken the correct steps in their eyes to get better, I still felt like I wore a scarlet letter as I walked around campus for the remainder of my time there. While the leadership knew my secret, I never spoke a word of it to anyone else. It was all vain work, and I kept my head down. But I kept telling myself that I was doing the right thing. And after you say something enough, you start to believe it, right?

I finished the program and prepared to come back home to the States. My parents and sister were actually planning to come spend the last week with me for graduation, but that was also the time when the avian flu caused a scare. The college cancelled our graduation and sent our diplomas in the mail. I changed my flight and left a few days early, out of caution; no one was sure what was going to happen. And I was ready to leave.

Upon my arrival back in the States in mid-July, I moved back in with my parents and my dad signed me up for biblical counseling where he was working at the time. The counseling center was on the campus of the local Bible college where my dad completed his master's degree. The college had a well-known program that specialized in biblical counseling. The only problem was that my dad was my therapist. However, I agreed to a session.

I remember pulling up to the counseling center for my first session. I whipped into a parking spot driving the purple-ish/blue 1998 four-door Honda civic I'd been gifted for my sixteenth birthday. I walked into the center and was greeted by the secretary, and then I took a seat in the waiting area. A few moments later, my dad walked into the room and motioned me back. He escorted me down the hall past several rooms with the doors closed until we arrived at an empty room. We entered, and he invited me to take a seat in a padded chair across the room. He then sat down a few feet away from me.

He crossed his legs, got out his notepad, clicked his pen, and asked me how I was doing. I told him that I was fine and that I was interested in learning more about how to control these urges I was having. He reiterated that I was doing the right thing and then proceeded to ask me more questions to get some background information about what led up to these thoughts and feelings.

I told him that through my life I'd always felt different. I felt like I was never understood, never heard, and looked at as weird. I told him that my attraction toward men wasn't something new. Rather, it was something I'd always had. But it had become more prominent the older and more mature I became.

I discussed how I never felt like I measured up to the man I was supposed to be. My brothers checked all of the boxes, so what was my problem?

My turmoil was internalized because of the Christian values that I'd been taught. This type of morality was etched into my thinking and influenced my worldview, which had a stake in everything. But the very person who I was, my personality, my heart, my emotions, the very core of my being blatantly contradicted my philosophy and integrity. How could I live with this dichotomy?

I was told that I needed to choose obedience to God's Word over wanting to please my fleshly desires. In other words, I needed to choose God over myself. But that meant I had to completely take myself out of the equation and somehow be someone else to fulfill my Christian duty. So that meant that I could never find love or have a physical relationship with a man because that would be unholy. Rather, a life of celibacy or marriage to a woman were the options left to me. Neither would work for me.

I was left with this impossible choice. The road map was given to me as if it was easy to arrive at the destination. No one had a clue how I was feeling or any idea what I was going through. But it was sure easy for them to show me Bible verses that seemed to make this very gray area black and white.

I completed one session with my dad. The awkwardness of spilling my deepest and darkest to my own father worked as an antithesis to the point of therapy. I didn't see a way of moving forward.

One night I was standing in the kitchen making General Tso's chicken and rice, and I told my dad that I felt cured of homosexuality, that I was no longer struggling, and that God worked a miracle. I would have said anything at the moment to get out of the most uncomfortable situation at the time. I know that I probably didn't fool him, but we both steered clear of the discomfort of further discussion. My mom and I never discussed the subject; she relegated that responsibility to my father. My siblings were oblivious to what was going on as they all had moved out, and we rarely spoke.

Despite being out to my parents, our relationship never changed. I was not treated differently, and I just knew that they wanted me to do the right thing according to the Bible. Their prayer was that I would not give in to my fleshly, gay desires.

I suppressed these unsettling feelings deep in the back of my brain. While they continued to torment me, it was easier to just not deal with it at the time. I had other things to focus on, like where I would go to college.

Chapter Ten

My next task was to figure out what I would do for the coming year. I knew I was headed to college, but I wasn't sure what I wanted to study. While I was in Argentina, I'd discovered that I enjoyed teaching English. I'd tutored some of the Hispanic students who were trying to learn English. So I looked into getting a degree in teaching English as a Second Language (TESL). Nursing remained in the back of my mind, but the TESL degree took precedence. I researched programs, but I'd missed most of the deadlines to start in the fall of 2009. I didn't want to miss another year of college, so I decided to stick with what I knew and enrolled at the college where my dad and sister had graduated. There, I would earn a Bible certificate and complete my Gen-Ed courses.

As I settled in to my college routine, I started looking for opportunities to get involved as a student. I noticed that auditions for the chorale would be held within the following days, so I signed up. I arrived at the music hall for the auditions and met several other people anxiously waiting to be called. As I heard my name, I entered into a music room where the choir director and his wife, Tim and Michelle Hontz, welcomed me with kind smiles. We discussed my background in music, and I sang a few basic scales. I was then tested on sight reading short portions of preselected music and ended by singing a verse of "Amazing Grace." They thanked me for coming and escorted me out of the room. A few days later, I was notified that I'd been selected to join the chorale for that year. I was elated to get back into music. And singing in a college chorale was extra special. I thought, *I'm in the big leagues now.*

Chorale was a highlight of my time in college. The directors showed such passion and excellence in music. They taught us well and instilled in each member a sense of pride of being a part of the chorale. We worked hard, practiced a lot, and had fun. Singing in a choir created a community that built unity among each of the members as we made music together. Chorale became a place to relieve stress. And the powerful balm of music provided an oasis for my turbulent heart.

We sang mostly sacred pieces in the chorale. The directors also sprinkled in some American folk songs and African spirituals to add variety. Some of my favorite spirituals were "Poor, Wayfaring Stranger" and the traditional spiritual "Keep Your Lamps Trimmed and Burning." I enjoyed these spirituals because of their deep-rooted meaning. They sent a message and provided a link of hope in an otherwise heinous time. Along with the message, I loved the rhythms, beats, and arrangements of these pieces. They were fun and dramatic. The vocal ranges were wide and challenging. I always got goose bumps when the sopranos hung on their high notes.

Based off my audition, Mr. Hontz placed me in the tenor section, which is what I sang in high school. At our first rehearsal, I remember walking into a large room. My eyes went right to the giant, black grand piano on the other side of the room. It was gorgeous. I wanted to run across the room and see it up close, but I refrained. At the center of the room was a small podium with a three-ring binder of music that I assumed was for the director. Directly across from that was a three-level platform with forty chairs set up in four different sections with two aisles down the middle. I found my seat, which was in between two other guys who had arrived before me. The guy to my left introduced himself, "Hi, my name is Michael. It's great to have you."

And the guy to my right said, "Hey, I'm Tony. It's great to meet you."

What friendly, people, I thought.

We engaged in small talk where I found out these two guys were sophomores in the music program. I told them that I was obviously new but excited to join the chorale.

Mr. and Mrs. Hontz walked in and introduced themselves, and then we started rehearsing. Mr. Hontz led us in a few exercise warm-ups before jumping right into a song we'd be performing at the fall concert. I don't remember which song we sang; however, I do remember hearing

Michael's voice and being completely awestruck. It was similar to Mandy Patinkin's voice in *The Secret Garden*. It was that rich, clear, tenor voice that carried but didn't overpower the rest of the group. For a moment, I had to stop and listen as he sang.

I also heard Tony sing. He had this fullness and resonance to his voice making it mature and controlled. I felt incredibly intimidated to be singing in between these—in my mind—professionals. I thought I was pretty good back in high school, but I realized that I had a lot to learn.

After that rehearsal, I still couldn't get over Michael's voice. I immediately got out my phone and called Alyssa, who I'd kept in contact with.

"Alyssa, you'll never believe what I'm about to tell you," I said.

"Tell me," she exclaimed.

"OK, get ready," I teased. "Remember *The Secret Garden*? Well, the guy who sat next to me in chorale has literally the same voice as Archibald."

"No way," she said

"Yes. It's incredible. I feel like it's too good to be true. These people are amazing."

"That's awesome. But you're amazing too. Enjoy it," she said in an encouraging and triumphant tone.

Throughout the rest of that year, I became good friends with both Michael and Tony. As we got to know one another, we found common areas of interest, most notably, music. But not only sacred music—we all loved Broadway. We spent hours together discussing and listening to musicals such as *Hairspray*, *The Color Purple*, and *Jekyll & Hyde*, to name a few. Michael had purchased some of the songbooks, so we'd spend time in the music rooms, singing parts and acting out scenes. One of our favorite songs to sing was the powerhouse duet "In His Eyes" from *Jekyll & Hyde*. They were women's parts, but we didn't care. And it was refreshing not to worry about being reprimanded for playing a woman's part.

Musical theatre allowed me to put on a mask. I could sing songs about what I felt inside without anyone knowing the reason behind it. I sang songs like "On My Own" from *Les Miserables* or "In His Eyes" thinking about a male crush I had or someone I wished I could confess my feelings to but couldn't. And there was one such individual who will remain anonymous that took residence in my heart. Every look from him gave me butterflies in my stomach. When he spoke to me, the sound of his voice made the little hairs on my body stand up. I thought of him always, and I kept these feelings locked in a vault deep within my soul. I'd play the scenes in my mind as if they were real. I'd dream of him choosing me. I saw him walking me to class hand-in-hand. When we arrived to the classroom door, he'd give me a kiss as he said, "See you after class." And during the lecture I would only think of him. We dined together. And our days and nights were consumed with the intoxicating warmth of his presence. I ached that we could not be together.

I wished I could be honest, but I kept the burden of the truth to myself. And the truth would remain hidden because the utopia that I created in my mind was a sin-sick fantasy. I felt alone. I felt like there could not possibly be anyone else like me dealing with this same-sex attraction. It was too evil. So I kept my secret buried in the songs I sang.

The friendship I made in college broke down the social construct of toxic masculinity that had been haunting me throughout the years. These guys enjoyed music, reading, sharing afternoon tea, and sitting around gossiping about the latest fashion. I'd never been able to do this before with other guys. I felt like I could be myself, and no one made me feel bad about it—that is, until one day I was sitting in health class, which was taught by one of the athletic personnel, whom my family and I knew well from the years we spent there previously. Not only did we go to the same church, but also my dad worked with him during the time we'd lived there.

This individual had known me growing up and therefore had seen my feminine tendencies. As we were sitting in class one day, he began to talk about gender roles and how they correlated with biblical values. He talked about how women belong in the home and men belong outside of the home. He said that women do the cooking, cleaning, and laundry while men take care of mowing the lawn, chopping wood, and working on the cars.

Then he singled me out in front of the whole class and said, "Jordan, now what would you do if you had a flat tire and couldn't call your brothers or your dad to help you?"

Stunned by this question, I simply replied, "I don't know."

"See," he said, "we as men need to know how to perform these basic tasks in the event that we would need to. And by doing these things, we build our masculinity."

I slid down in my chair and slouched forward in a cowardly way, embarrassed by what he could have meant by that comment.

But what he'd said was true. By his standard, the standard I'd grown up with, I wasn't fulfilling my role as a man. And it was a feeling of inadequacy that started long before this encounter but was solidified in this moment because someone else revealed it, not only to me but also to a classroom full of my peers.

I walked out of class feeling exposed, but when I walked into chorale rehearsal, those feelings were washed away by the melody of "Poor, Wayfaring Stranger" that we were working on that week. I redirected my focus onto the music and expressed myself through every line, crescendo, and decrescendo. While I felt like a wayfaring stranger, I also knew in my heart that life would eventually get better. I needed to hold on to hope.

Spending time with Michael and Tony also relieved the stress I felt from not fulfilling my Christian duty of being a man. We banded together like brothers. In the very back of my mind, I had thoughts that maybe, just maybe, these guys were gay as well. But I knew that Michael was married and Tony was a missionary kid from Uruguay. And we were at a Bible college where people went to study the Bible. While it was nice to have these liberating friendships, the Christian fundamentals remained intact. While I had my suspicions, I didn't mention anything. And my thoughts returned to the idea that no one was as wicked as I was. Oh yeah, and *Wicked* was another musical we loved to belt out between classes and rehearsals.

I wasn't about to bring up my history and relive the confession phase again. This was a place where no one knew me. This was a place where I could have a fresh start. I focused on not dealing with my moral instability and trying to be as Christian as I could. I prayed, read the Bible, and did my best to learn from my classes. And when I wasn't doing that, I hung out with my new friends as often as I could.

Michael and his wife lived in the student housing condos a few doors down from where my family and I lived previously. I knew the layout well. One of my favorite memories was going to Michael's each week to watch the newest episode of the TV show *Glee*. We loved the show so much that our friend group dressed up as the main characters in Glee for one of the days during Spirit Week that year. I was voted to dress up as Will Schuester, as I was typically already seen in a sweater and button-down, collared shirt. I was surprised that I wasn't chosen to go as Kurt (the openly gay student), as we were probably the most alike, but I was also relieved that my friends didn't place me in that box. Furthermore, dressing up as a gay character in a conservative, Christian college would have created quite a negative buzz.

We all acknowledged Kurt as a character, but no one brought up his lifestyle. It was like the elephant in the room that no one talked about. For me, I knew that I identified with Kurt on many levels as he was gay, dealt with bullies and lived a life where he was different than his peers. The difference between Kurt and me was that I wasn't ready to accepted myself. Being gay felt like having a stain on my heart that I couldn't wash off no matter how hard I'd tried. There was a tiny part of me that wished for a life where I could be freely myself, but I wasn't ready for it. It still felt wrong to want that. So I tried to do the right thing and ignore it.

As I settled in to college, my parents were still living in Pennsylvania. They were an eight-hour drive from the college, so I mostly saw them during breaks. Though, I would get the occasional phone call to check in and provide an update on how things were going. We never discussed anything about my struggles during these phone calls or visits. But I know they were relieved that I chose to attend a Bible college where I would be kept safe in a conservative bubble, away from the temptations of the world. My sister and her husband lived in Charleston, which was an hour away from where I was. I spent many weekends with them to get a break from dorm life and also enjoy a home-cooked meal. We'd often play board or card games and watch movies like Rocket Man or Cool Runnings. Both my sister and brother-in-law were unaware of my struggles at this time. I kept it well-hidden. My goal was to remain as pious on the outside as I could. It was the best way to avoid questions. I was accepted as long as I appeared Christian.

A few months before the school year ended, Mr. Hontz approached me to talk about my future plans. I'd told him that I was planning on transferring to another college the following year. I still hadn't decided between TESL or nursing. Mr. Hontz respected my decision but encouraged me to think about staying and joining the music program the following year as a music major. I was humbled by his kindness, and assured him I would think (and most importantly, pray) about it.

Over the following weeks, I pondered what had been said about joining the music program. I loved music and singing, but did I love it enough to invest a degree in it? Music gave me hope by providing an outlet that no other activity did, so I decided to go for it.

The following day, I informed Mr. Hontz of my decision. He gave me a big, solid handshake and welcomed me to the program. Later that day, I filled out the application to transfer into the music program. My acceptance letter came a few days later. I relayed the news to my parents. They congratulated my decision and expressed their joy that I chose to stay within a Christian environment.

"I know that God is going to do great things through you," my mom said over the phone as we ended our conversation.

That summer of 2010, I took summer classes to get caught up in the music program so I could graduate within three years. I took voice lessons as well as an introductory music class, which Mr. Hontz taught. I was the only one in the class that summer, so we had a lot of one-on-one time that allowed us to delve into the material. He was an extraordinary teacher; I soaked up every minute and gleaned as much as I could from the knowledge he selflessly and humbly gave. We spent much time together discussing music. He spent extra time coaching me and teaching me how to be a better singer.

Voice lessons were the highlight of my week. I loved learning the proper techniques of singing and how to sing with a stronger, higher, and more controlled voice. I practiced every day, which resulted in small improvements from week to week. It was satisfying to work toward something and achieve goals. Furthermore, I funneled my stress through the music and labeled it as expression. It was the most cleansing exercise I was able to do.

In voice lessons, I was taught that music is all about movement and imagery. We moved to eliminate tightness, and we used imagery to improve our sound and quality. For example, one way to keep the sound open and full is to imagine having an egg in the mouth as one sings. We want the jaw to be loose, the tongue down, and the soft palate lifted in order to maintain an open, bright sound that carries all the way to the back of the room. As we breathed using the diaphragm, we imagined smelling a bouquet of roses or chocolate chip cookies baking in the oven. We stood firmly on the balls of our feet as if they were nailed to the floor, knees slightly bent, shoulders back, and arms hanging loosely at the sides. During lessons, I moved my arms and body in all directions to facilitate a relaxed sound. I can't imagine how ridiculous I looked, but the actions worked. Through these silly movements, I was training my body to sing, and it was fun. Every time I sang, I created something. I imagined something. I entered a world beyond my reality, and it was cathartic.

Throughout the next three years, I grew into my part as a tenor. Each spring break, the chorale went on tour to different churches, advertising the college and performing the concert we had prepared. During that week, we traveled to different states and had the chance to meet many different people. Some of the members at each of the churches we visited opened up their homes to host us for the night. Normally, we went in pairs. We never knew what kind of home we would be staying in until we pulled into the driveway and went inside.

I remember one time my friend and I were riding in the back seat of our host's car as they drove us from the church to their house. These car rides were always filled with the same small talk questions like, "Where are you from?" "What are you studying?" "What do you plan on doing after you graduate?" Sometimes, I wished we could just hand them a note card with all of our information on it. While I enjoyed talking and getting to know all these different people, there were many times I just wanted to rest my voice.

Perhaps the most memorable chorale tour was during my senior year. I was able to sing a powerhouse duet with my good friend Leslee eight times that week. Leslee sang soprano. She was only five foot five but could soar to the high notes while making it look effortless. She had the voice of an angel, and when she talked, she had a Southern twang you never noticed when she sang. She had the type of tone and resonance that would carry her voice all the way to the back of the room. She reminded me of Kristin Chenoweth with both her height and her vocal range. Leslee wasn't in the music program, but she invested a lot of time in the chorale. Music brought us together as we shared many laughs and memorable times over McDonald's sweet tea.

The duet we sang was called "Above All Else." This was a triumphant, upbeat ballad that closed the show. The piano accompaniment was advanced, the harmony was tight, and the range challenged me more than any other sacred song I sang. And the purposefully placed key changes added color and excitement to carry out the themes of triumph and adoration. I looked forward to singing that piece mostly because for three minutes and fifty-eight seconds I was transported to the musical oasis I'd created. As I sang, I forsook this desolate place, and the only thing that brought me back was the applause of the audience.

During my senior year of college, I submitted a request to the dean of students about having my own dorm room instead of sharing one. This was a common request among seniors. The dean answered my inquiry with a follow-up question *Why do you want your own room?* I answered by saying that I wanted my own space to study and prepare for my senior recital. I felt like I was old enough and proved myself godly enough to have my own room. The dean replied and said that due to my behavior over the last three years, involvement on campus and good recommendations from faculty, I would be granted my request of occupying my own room for my senior year.

I was elated by the news. In the back of my mind, I knew the temptations that awaited me, but I vowed to God that I would remain holy and work hard not to sin. We were taught that if we loved God, then we wouldn't make a habit of sinning. Over time, though, my double standard of living took control.

Many nights, my hormones would start acting up, and I'd get the urge to satisfy my feelings. I'd climb into bed with my phone and scroll through images and videos of men, being careful to keep it to myself.

There was a "lights out" rule that went into effect at 10:00 PM. Around 10:05 PM, the RA went around to the rooms, opened the door slightly and made sure everyone was in bed with the lights out and no electronics. Even though I had my own room, I still had to follow the rule. I could usually hear the quiet opening and closing of doors, so around that time, I'd put away my phone and wait for my door to open. Once it closed, I'd get my phone back out and continue where I left off.

I remember one evening sitting in my room before lights out casually scrolling questionable material on my phone when suddenly my friend— who was the head RA—came bursting through my door with an enthusiastic, "Hello!"

I almost threw my phone across the room as we both locked eyes for a few seconds. Luckily, I was covered, but I was afraid he'd seen my heart pounding outside my chest.

"wha...what...what's up?" I said as I remained seated in the chair with my hand over my lap.

"Just bringing back the shirt I borrowed." He said.

Terrified of getting up off the chair, I told him to place it on the bed, which he did. We shared an awkward "see ya later" and never spoke of the encounter. We are friends to this day, and I still don't know if he knew what I was in the middle of, but perhaps he will now if he reads this.

I didn't enjoy this hypocritical lifestyle, but I also didn't know how to not be attracted to men. How does one live in the world as a human being without thinking about or feeling a physical attraction towards another person? It's in our genetic makeup to have these desires, but mine was unacceptable. That which was supposed to be normal was an abomination. Being told I shouldn't have feelings for men felt like being told I shouldn't have feelings. I felt like I couldn't be human. I had two identities—being Christian and being gay. The two did not mix. And I felt sacrificed in the crossfire.

I wanted so badly to be freed from this inward torment I felt but kept it inside so that people saw the version of myself that I wanted them to see. But this was not sustainable behavior.

During my senior year of college, I had two things on my mind: my senior voice recital and graduation. I worked tirelessly on my recital. Essentially, this event took everything I'd worked on and learned over the past four years and showcased it. And it was my ticket to earning a music degree.

I loved putting the show together. I was given requirements to sing pieces from different periods, but I was able to choose which songs I wanted to sing. The music I chose excited me. Upon my introduction to music, I had taken an immediate liking to Romanticism and Impressionism. I identified with these time periods because the music was dramatic. The chords were lush, the sounds full, and the progressions emotional. I felt connected to this type of music as my heart beat to the same rhythm of what had been written in the music. I felt every high and low; each rapid change from major and minor key synced to my inner thoughts and feelings. One minute I could be happy and then next paralyzed with depression stemming from a place so deep only music could know.

I enjoyed singing pieces from Mahler because of his rich, dark, and dramatic sound. I sang ten songs total including a few sacred pieces and, of course, a selection from Broadway. The musical theater choice I picked was "If I Can't Love Her" from *Beauty and the Beast*. I felt alive on stage that night. Performing under the spotlight was euphoric and exuberating. The music charged me with emotional delight as I heard my voice ricochet from the walls of the music hall. It felt like home. At the end of the concert, my parents were invited up to the stage for recognition and photos. When they arrived on stage, we shared a hug and they stood next to me. I could see a sparkle in my dad's eye as he fought back tears. I knew my parents were proud of me.

People congratulated me for weeks to come. I was humbled, grateful, and flattered by the acceptance from my peers. It was something I'd wanted for a long time, and I'd finally found a way to bridge the gap between my peers and me. My voice was that bridge.

Even though I had found a home within music, I was still left with burning questions about the war happening beneath the façade I had built. Surely there is more to life than merely living in a dream. One should be able to express himself openly, right? I knew that there had to be more to life than living in hiding.

Chapter Eleven

ible college had been the best place to mask my sexuality with biblical living. I learned through my Bible classes that the holier we lived, the better Christians we became. For that reason, my Christian worldview had quickly turned into a works-based Christianity, even though I claimed salvation was by grace alone. I'd sat in my classes listening to my professors preach about how the world would know us by our works (Matthew 7:16). They said that when we became saved, the Holy Spirit took up residence in our hearts and transformed our lives. Because of this miraculous work, our desires to sin should be exchanged for our wants to please the Lord with our lives. We shouldn't continue sinning. Rather, we should choose to serve the Lord with our lives (Romans 6). In fact, they had said that those who continued to live in sin probably weren't saved and should examine their hearts lest they be headed for the gates of hell. My struggle with faith hadn't changed, and I still didn't have that incredible testimony.

One of the most difficult concepts I had been taught was the doctrine of election, which introduced the idea that not all people are chosen to go to heaven. The human race is blinded by sin, not understanding their need for salvation unless the Holy Spirit opens their eyes and softens their hearts to want to know Jesus. And not everyone will have this desire. This doctrine was very uncomfortable for me. How could God create some people, already having chosen them to spend eternity with him and then others to spend eternity in hell? At the same time, the Bible makes it clear that anyone can be saved and no one is out of the reach of redemption. So what if I wasn't chosen to go to heaven, especially since I was dealing with same-sex attraction? Did my sin exempt me from grace?

My peers and I were in constant competition about who appeared the godliest by how we acted, prayed, preached, and read the Bible. This perpetual battle to be number one instilled in me a false Christianity. Furthermore, I was taught to hate myself even more for who I was (a homosexual) because it went against my beliefs. I was taught to deny myself because what was inside of me was sin, and it controlled me. Everything I was taught not to do was the core of my very being. I was constantly at war with my own soul over something I couldn't change. I wanted to do what was right, but I kept sinning, and I didn't understand why. Because of my habitual sinning, I was afraid I wasn't going to heaven; rather, I was terrified of burning in hell for forever. 1 John 3:6-9 says that those who are saved will not keep sinning, rather, their salvation will be evident through their righteousness. So, where did that leave me? Is it even possible to be a Christian homosexual? I grappled with this question through the following years. This question turned into agony as it leeched onto me while it slowly sucked the life out of my soul. This theme will be explained in more detail in the coming chapters.

But what did the Bible say about homosexuality? Evangelicals were quick to throw verses around condemning homosexuality such as those from Leviticus and 1 Kings. However, the law was replaced with grace because of Christ's redemptive work on the cross. Those who trust in Him no longer fear death, but were given the gift of eternal life. The Messiah came and paid the ultimate price of the law for us.

Then they would say that God condemns homosexuality as well in the New Testament in the books of Romans, Mark, and Jude. But the problem I had was that all of these verses talk about frivolous sex, lust, rape, and prostitution. I didn't see the condemning of same-sex marriage or relationship that was based on love and desire for one another.

But despite all of this, everyone I knew and loved fervently preached against this kind of lifestyle. I didn't know what to believe. I just wanted to be a good person, but how was that possible?

Every day was a war that wreaked havoc on my soul. The rivalry within me grew bloodier and caused more stress and frustration than I can describe. These negative feelings affected my relationships and personal life on many levels. I became short tempered and easily frustrated. I would often snap at my friends or become antisocial but then feel left out if people wouldn't hang out with me. I was needy, but everyone annoyed me. I felt empty and lifeless. I felt like the more I sought God, the farther away He was. It was as if God was hiding from me. But I was still convinced that as long as I kept being as godly as I could, then my struggle would be abated. How wrong I was!

After I graduated, I felt lost. I moved back in with my parents in Pennsylvania as my friends embarked on their own journeys. All I had was a piece of paper with my degree on it and a mound of student debt I didn't know what to do with. And to be honest, there wasn't a big job market for music professionals.

One summer day, I received a message from one of my college friends, Sam, who was living in Peru as part of a study-abroad program. The program catered to college students in their junior and senior years. The program was sponsored by a mission board in the States, which was home to hundreds of missionaries sprinkled across the globe spreading the gospel of Christ around the world. There were several missionary families in Lima, so the mission built a school that served the missionary kids. The school followed the US school system so that when the students graduated, they could attend US colleges and universities with no educational delays.

The school needed teachers, so Sam reached out to me and asked if I might be interested in coming down for a year to teach at the high school. Intrigued, I looked into the school and the opportunities for me there. The problem was that this would be an unpaid position as it was run by missionaries who raised economic support from churches in the States as their income.

I prayed about this opportunity and decided to apply for the position. Within a few days, I heard back and was accepted. I also decided to apply to the mission board associated with the school to become an official missionary. I did this because I thought that the more Christian things I did, the more God would bless me and tame the moral conundrum inside my heart and mind. It may sound silly, but I was desperate to find relief. And if that meant being a missionary, then I would do it. My logic came from the teachings that the way we live our lives reflects our relationships with Christ. The Bible says that they will know us by our works.

The application process was long and in-depth. The board wanted to ensure that all of their prospective missionaries agreed with their theology and doctrine. But I knew the lingo they wanted to hear because I had a theology degree from a college that had a good relationship with this particular mission board. I used all the right words and theological phrases on my application to make it shine. I sent it off and heard back a few days later.

I was accepted as a new missionary, and I had about one month to raise my support. My stress was high. How was I going to raise around twelve thousand dollars to support myself for a year living in Peru? In reality, I didn't need much as housing was provided. And the cost of living was cheaper in Peru than the United States, but I was still overridden with anxiety of trying to find the minimum monetary support I needed. I immediately started calling churches, posting to Facebook, and writing letters to family and friends.

Within a short time, I'd raised several thousand dollars to support my ministry in Peru. I didn't have everything, but I had enough to get started. The mission board required its missionaries to have a certain percentage of their support pledged before they were allowed to leave for the field. I didn't hit my percentage goal because of my time constraint, but because the school needed teachers, I was permitted to leave. I didn't let my monetary deficit rob me of the joy of moving to a new country. Somewhere within me, I knew that I would be OK. I knew that money would come in, and I was willing to roll the dice to experience another adventure overseas.

So for the second time in my life, I packed my bags to move overseas. But this time, I was more excited, because I wasn't going as a student, I was going as a teacher. Teaching had been something that interested me for a long time, but I didn't know if I wanted to do it professionally. So, what better way to know if you like something than actually doing it? And living in Peru would provide me with the opportunity to grow my Spanish proficiency. So here I was packing up my life to move to a country I'd never been to before, to a culture I didn't understand, with money I didn't have, and teaching a subject I wasn't qualified to teach. What could go wrong?

PART
Two

Chapter Twelve

One early morning, my parents and I loaded up the car with two large suitcases weighing in at fifty pounds each and two carry-on items weighing as much as my suitcases. As the sun rose over the Shenandoah mountains, my parents drove me to Washington, DC, to catch a plane to Lima, Peru. Even though this wasn't my first move, it was still difficult to leave. Saying goodbye is rarely easy, but I have found it incredibly important to step out of your comfort zone; there you will find growth. My parents were very supportive of my moving to Peru as a missionary. They were proud of the decisions I was making because they aligned with what they had dedicated their lives to teach us—to follow the Lord. After a long, uneventful flight, I felt the plane start the initial descent and the captain came over the PA system, announcing our arrival into Lima.

As we neared the ground, I looked out the window and saw the city I would soon call home. It was dark, so all I saw was a trail of pale-yellow street lights scattered throughout the terrain. I felt excitement and apprehension. The wheels of the Boeing 777 gently touched down on the runway as we were all thrust forward at the touch of the brakes. The engines revved loudly and then quieted to a gentle purr. We made a big turn and taxied to our gate. The flight attendants came over the PA saying, "Damas y caballeros, bienvenidos a Lima. La hora local son las 2330. Esperamos que hayan disfrutado de su viaje y gracias por elegir United Airlines."

And once again in English, "Ladies and gentlemen, welcome to Lima. The local time is 11:30 p.m. We hope that you enjoyed your flight and thank you for choosing United Airlines."

I made it.

It took a couple of hours to get through customs, but I received a tourist visa. I found my bags at the carousel and walked toward the entrance door where I saw a missionary couple waiting for me to take me back to the place I would be staying. They were career missionaries who had spent their adult lives working in Peru. I thought they were the neatest people not only because they were culturally diverse and fluent in Spanish, but also because they were missionaries. What a life. What a reputation.

Around 3:00 a.m., we arrived at the house where I'd be staying, which was on the same lot as the school where I'd be teaching. I was high on adventure and began to unpack. The school where I would be teaching was set on a corner in a very nice, gated community. The school owned a spacious lot surrounded with a high brick wall. Within was the school and several apartments where the teachers, administrator, and groundskeeper lived. It was a beautiful spot. There were two palm trees that stood tall in front of the school, and I thought, *I have always wanted palm trees in my front yard, and now I do.*

The next day, I was pleasantly greeted by my college friends, Sam and Rachel. It was great having them around to help acclimate me to the culture. It was also nice to see familiar faces, especially when culture shock and homesickness set in—a luxury I didn't have in Argentina.

That first morning, Sam and Rachel accompanied me on my first trip to the Peruvian grocery store. We took the public transit to get there. And was I ever in for a surprise. In Peru, safety measures are arbitrary, and traffic laws are more like guidelines than enforced rules. The three of us very white Americans walked about three-quarters of a mile to the street to wait for the right bus to board. My eyes widened as I noticed buses passing by, bulging with people. There were some buses that had passengers literally hanging out the front door. More bodies meant more money to the bus owners, so if they could fit, they could ride.

Finally, our ride approached, and the guy collecting money waved for us to get on. I didn't know where we would fit, but we squeezed our way on. It was hot, sweaty, and uncomfortable. But this was the new normal I would have to get used to. It took time, but I acclimated.

We arrived at the grocery store safe and sound, though my head was still spinning from what I'd just experienced. I perused the aisles, taking notice of all of the Peruvian products and dishes I couldn't wait to try.

Getting around on the buses was economical, but it required a lot of learning. They didn't always have designated stops like in the States, so it was important to know where you were going and the street names of where you wanted to stop. When I approached my destination, I would yell, "Baja!" as I pushed my way through to the front and exited the bus.

I arrived in Peru shortly before the start of the school year. Those few days consisted of meeting my coworkers, setting up my classroom, and studying materials rigorously to prepare for my first day of classes teaching middle and high school English and literature. I struggled a great deal trying to come up with lesson plans for the semester. How did one plan out an entire semester when each day would surely present its own agenda and challenges? Completely lost and frustrated, I reached out to some of my education friends who I had met in college for advice on how to make this first semester go smoothly. Some of the best advice I was given was this: always give the students a fresh start. In other words, every time you see them, treat it as if it's the first time. Let go of issues from the past and treat them with love and kindness no matter what.

I went to bed the night before classes with butterflies in my stomach. I tossed and turned repeatedly waking up and checking the time. My alarm clock finally sounded at 6:15 a.m. Normally, I struggled to get up in the morning, but my first-day jitters and adrenaline sprung me from bed without a complaint. I wore my signature Will Schuester look, a pair of dress pants, and a sweater vest over a button-down collared shirt.

Classes started at 8:00 a.m. I walked over to the school with coffee in hand and entered my classroom around 7:30 a.m. I looked over some notes one last time before stepping out and waiting for the kids to arrive.

The school had two floors. The first one had the elementary classrooms, and the second consisted of the high school classrooms and a chapel. The hallway and the staircase were outside. And the doors of the classroom opened to greet the sun rays beaming down from the bright, open sky. In front of the school was a large yard and a small building that made up the library. To the right of the library was a basketball court.

I stood toward the middle of the staircase and watched as the kids wandered in. They all made their way to the basketball court (*la cancha*) where they greeted each other with smiles and told stories about their summers. As the bell rang, the kids lined up outside in front of the flag pole to pledge allegiance to the American flag and to be led in prayer by the interim administrator. When prayer ended, the kids made their way to their own classrooms.

I remember that first day the high school students asked me where I came from and what my credentials were. Telling them I had a music degree didn't instill any confidence. They wanted to know what authority I had to be teaching English. They wanted to be able to trust me, and I wasn't giving them any reason to. Had I made a mistake?

The middle school students were much easier to win over. Middle schoolers are still of that age where apathy hasn't set in yet and they still have their elementary innocence. They laughed at my silly jokes and went along with the change that happened that year. I looked forward to teaching these boys and girls even though they were rowdy and full of energy. It took quite a bit of discipline to control them every day, but it was fun and grew easier with time.

Every day was the same. I woke up early, struggled to win the hearts of the kids, went home, and studied for hours to prepare for the next day. I felt like I was failing, not only myself but also the students. My high school students slouched in their chairs and stared at me as I fumbled through the lessons. Their judgmental looks and apathetic attitudes made me want to crawl under a rock, but I was there to do a job, and I wanted to do it well. Most of all, I wanted the students to like me. But how?

Every day, I begged God for the grace to walk through my classroom door. It took every ounce of energy and hope I had within me to make it through each day. But every morning, I woke up and showed up with the materials I'd prepared for the day.

During those first couple of weeks, I was in search of a church to attend. The mission board I was with required its missionaries to find a church to serve in, so that's what I did. My friend Rachel was attending a small church called Iglesia Bautista de Musa. Musa was the next town over just a few miles from where I was living. I attended the church a couple of times, met with the pastor, and decided this would be the place I would attend during my time in Peru.

I chose that church for a couple of reasons. First, Rachel attended there. She not only was a familiar presence, but she also helped acclimate me to the church and introduced me to the members there. Second, I wanted to get involved with music. Since Rachel and I studied in the music program together in the States, it was easy to transition into a musical role at the church. Finally, this church had many young adults my age who I looked forward to getting to know. There was one guy in the group named Daniel who caught my eye. I'll leave whether or not he influenced my vote to the reader.

Little by little, the students began to warm up to me. Rapport established itself as I committed to being genuine and showed them I was there for them, not just as their teacher but as a friend. I worked hard to make class fun and memorable.

First, I made an open-door policy. I was always available to my students, whether it was during school hours or not. I remember several times video chatting with my students after the day was over (with parents present) about class materials and concepts they weren't understanding. I loved teaching. I loved giving my time to help. Most of all, I loved seeing the light bulb come on and the smile that appeared as they understood something they'd previously had trouble with. I loved watching my students grow.

Second, I tried to make the subject matter as pragmatic as possible. If you can get students to believe in the work they're doing, then they will apply themselves so much more than if they were doing busywork. And I'd learned that from Mr. Hontz. Every project that he made us do was worthwhile and purposeful. The most memorable was a digital music library with completed PowerPoint slides we made for ourselves to be used in future church ministry or any other music program we may be in, which I ended up using in Peru.

So while reading the classics like *Paradise Lost*, works by Shakespeare, and so on, I made it fun and interactive. We delved into the material, and we studied the authors. Instead of just reading the plays, I handed out the parts, and we acted it out. The kids loved overdramatizing the love between *Romeo and Juliet* or getting very theatrical with the fight scenes and dying in *King Lear*. I got a few knocks on the door from other teachers to keep the noise down.

I also made two other adaptations to the material that I was teaching. First, I created a writing seminar to prepare the kids for college writing and research. For my juniors and seniors, I thought about what would be most helpful to them as they prepared for college. My mind kept going back to one thing—writing. I wanted my students to learn how to write well to prepare them for college. I reached out to another professor and missionary at a neighbor school who had a master's degree in English. Together we developed a writing workshop for the students, which guided them through the process of writing and preparing a research paper. She taught the majority of the material as she was the expert. I helped with the writing process, and we both graded the term papers. The kids did a great job, and I hope they learned a lot. Most of all, I hope they were better prepared for college as a result.

Second, I created a Bible curriculum to use. At the time, I believed that the Bible and Christian living were paramount to successful living. When I received the provided materials for the Bible class, they looked like they had been hand-me-downs used over the decades. They reminded me of something you would learn in a Sunday school class. It was fluff and required nothing from the students. They already knew the stories. They already knew the right answers. I wanted to shake up their thinking. I wanted to make them question their beliefs and find answers. I wanted to rock their world by asking the tough questions and discussing the answers. So I packed up those old, crinkled papers, and I began to work on something that I thought would be much more beneficial and engaging for the students.

I wanted to teach the kids to think for themselves and to adopt Christianity for themselves because they believed in it, not because someone else told them to. While I was more liberal in my thinking than they were, I was also still very much in denial, living my hypocritical lifestyle. Nonetheless, I worked tirelessly to live a godly life because I believed that was the only way to tame the homosexual warfare within me.

Life in Peru wasn't just about the teaching. I wanted to know the Peruvian people, the culture, the food, and I desired to enhance my Spanish skills. I made it a point to have a life outside of the classroom. I mean, how often do you get to live in another country? I was excited. But I had to gain the courage to go out and make friends. Perhaps I could do that through music. Or maybe I could try to get a girlfriend?

Chapter Thirteen

The young adult group at the church accepted me with open arms. We normally met on Saturday nights for small group and Bible study. There were usually about twenty people in attendance on the regular. Of those twenty, about ten of us hung out on a steady basis. And I thought some of the guys in the group were cute, so while I enjoyed growing our friendships, I also took advantage of the opportunities to hang out with my innocent boy crushes.

When we got together, we enjoyed playing board games like Ticket to Ride (thank God there were rules in Spanish), go out to eat for pollo a la brasa, which is traditional Peruvian grilled chicken, or host movie nights. The group loved to watch horror movies, so one night, I invited them over to my apartment, set up a projector, and streamed *El Conjuro* (*The Conjuring*), which is still one of my favorite horror films. My Spanish grew by leaps and bounds because none of my friends spoke English with the exception of Rachel. But we spoke in Spanish to each other when around other Peruvians.

I also started to get more involved in music at the church. They had no one to lead music, so I volunteered to fill that role. Because Rachel studied piano performance in college, she was the obvious choice for accompanying the church music. We worked together on improving the music at the church. From then on, every Sunday I led music at the church in Spanish. I also introduced the use of PowerPoint to the pastor so the words could be projected onto the screen instead of using hymnals. This would also allow the use of other songs besides just hymns. We bought a projector and started to use it. That nifty project Mr. Hontz had us do in college also came into use as I pulled a lot of PowerPoint presentations to use in the song sets I'd created for Sunday morning worship.

There was a big interest in learning music at the church. Before, the members just sang the same songs over and over again, which became very routine and lost a lot of sentiment. Now, they were able to learn more contemporary songs like "Come, Now Is the Time to Worship," "Jesus Messiah," "How Great Is Our God," and "What a Beautiful Name," among others. And there was excitement surrounding that.

I also started a choir for those who were interested, including several of the young adults whom I'd come to know. In total, there were about twenty people who joined the choir. We didn't sing anything too complicated. For the most part, we sang hymns they were familiar with, and then I presented newer songs like the ones previously mentioned. We usually sang in two parts, and sometimes I would sing a third. I taught them the use of vowels in chorale singing and how to listen to each other. They sing as one sound—no one is supposed to overpower the other. And this was all done in Spanish. I remember going home every night being mentally exhausted from translating in my mind all day long. I felt like Gloria (Sofia Vergara) in *Modern Family* when she gets upset with her husband for not understanding how difficult it is for her to constantly translate and communicate after she learned English when her native tongue is Spanish.

I did my best to play the good Christian part with my heavy involvement at church and the school. But my hopes of becoming godlier and therefore less homosexual didn't work out as planned. It didn't take long for me to discover that the Wi-Fi signal reached my apartment across the yard from where the router was in the school office. The signal was weak, but still worked. To relax my mind from translating and teaching, I'd open up my smartphone and make salacious searches into the night. Then I would wake up the next morning and either head to church or step into the classroom where I was viewed as a model servant of Jesus Christ.

The kids loved to grab my phone and hide it or take photos with it. Sometimes I forgot to delete the pages I'd visited or images I'd seen the night before. Noticing they had possession of my phone and the content therein, I'd grab the phone back in a panic and instruct them that this was personal property and boundaries must be set. I imagined the horror of one of them discovering the risqué content I'd viewed. And that thought delivered a numbing feeling that shot through my body. However, I thank God that things were left unseen.

I knew what I was doing was wrong. At the end of every night, I'd fall to my knees in prayer asking God to forgive me for my fleshly choices. I felt an uncontrollable pang in my heart from committing the same sin over and over again, but I also wanted to see more. I wasn't out meeting guys in Peru, so I hid this part of my life behind closed doors. I knew I was playing with fire, but I didn't stop.

When word got out that I had a music degree, I was asked to take charge of the high school choir. I happily acquiesced to the request. I was eager to engage with music and teach what I'd learned in college. A fellow colleague, Sarah, who taught the elementary kids, agreed to play the piano while I led the choir. Our friendship blossomed the more we worked on music together. Sarah had a great musical ear and impeccable rhythm. I was lucky to have her on the piano, especially at a small Christian school in Lima, Peru.

Per the norm, most of the students were rather apathetic about being a part of the choir. The music they sang in the past hadn't resonated with them. No wonder they grudgingly came to choir and sang without any passion. I made it my mission to change that. I wanted them to love singing and love being a part of a choir. I wanted to give them a reason to enjoy singing and something to be proud of.

We started our rehearsals with warm-ups, and I gave them reasons for the exercises we did. Everything had a purpose. We not only learned the music on the page, but I taught them musical techniques to enhance and improve their sound. They learned to work together, listen to each other, and create something beautiful with one another. Being a part of a choir is being a part of a community. It builds trust and deepens relationships. We analyzed the music together and rehearsed it bit by bit until it became a work they could be proud of.

We sang both contemporary and sacred songs. I took their suggestions and adapted them to what we could do in our concert. From choir, I started teaching individual voice lessons to those who had interest and showed potential. I worked with two specific students who impressed me with their potential. One was a soprano, and the other was a tenor. I spent extra time with these two students as they held the choir together. For the Christmas concert, I sang a duet with the tenor called "It Was a Starry Night" by David and Bonnie Huntsinger, which was one of the highlights of my time in Peru. I knew this song from singing it one year in college at the Christmas program.

Sarah and I spent a lot of time working on music together. And our time with each other developed into a beautiful friendship. She was a pastor's kid from southern Florida and ended up in Peru as a missionary a few years before I arrived. She was Cuban, and she grew up speaking Spanish. Her personality was bubbly, and she had this infectious laugh that carried through the room. She was intelligent and a good Christian lady. I started to invite her to my church in Musa, even though she was attending her own church at the time. She did come a few times to help with music, and she also came to show her support when I was asked to do a short teaching series on the role of music in the church. When I was teaching, I'd love to see her in the congregation nodding along with an approving and encouraging smile. Looking out at her from the stage, I'd think, *Is she interested in me? I mean, who spends this much time helping out another person if there are no other underlying feelings involved?* I let the thought oscillate in my mind over the next few weeks. I also started to invite her to hang out with my friends and me from Musa whenever we hung out. And our friend group grew by one member.

The closer Sarah and I became, the more I started to think about whether I could get into a relationship with her, especially if she had the same thoughts as I did. Could a relationship help defeat the struggle within? I'd dated girls in high school, but none of it had helped; maybe since I was older and more mature, things would be different this time? And since our relationship would be Christ-centered, perhaps my struggle would take a back seat, and I wouldn't have to deal with it anymore. I analyzed this possibility over and over again.

Since one of the things we did to relax was host movie nights, we often invited our Musa friends. We would order in from Las Canastas which served some of the best pollo a la brasa in Lima. It was suggested that we watch *Pearl Harbor* one night, which I happily agreed to saying, "Yeah! I enjoy a war movie." But let's be honest, I only wanted to watch it for Ben Affleck and Josh Hartnett.

As my first year of teaching came to an end, I was torn about whether or not I should stay another year or go back to the States. I'd been asked to extend my contract, and I'd developed a great relationship with my students. I was getting more involved in the community and with the church I was attending. I was becoming much more comfortable with the culture, public transportation, and making more friends. Was I ready to leave? Would I have enough money to stay? I spent the next several weeks weighing the pros and cons, making spreadsheets, and seeking counsel.

I had a lengthy conversation with one of the missionaries I'd met and whose kids I taught. During our talk, I told him that I was worried about money, but I would love to stay. He told me that I shouldn't let fear of money deter me from staying or rob me of experiences. He told me that the money would come in.

I put together a prayer letter and a short PowerPoint presentation highlighting what I was doing in Peru. The purpose of this was to send it to local churches in the United States requesting monetary support of my ministry in Peru. I sent it to the churches I was affiliated with, and Sarah was a big help by helping me send out letters to churches in Southern Florida where her family was.

At the end of the school year, I returned home to Virginia where my parents were living. They had moved there from Pennsylvania during my first year in Peru. I stayed for a few weeks to visit with family and go to some of the churches I'd sent my letter to, including the church I'd attended in West Virginia while I was in college. A few of the pastors gave me a ten-minute spot during the Sunday morning service to present my ministry in Peru, discuss what God was doing there, and ask for support to continue what was happening there.

I then flew down to Florida to meet with Sarah and visit some of the churches she knew. While there, I met her parents and family. They showed me around Fort Lauderdale and then introduced me to a few churches. First, I went to Sarah's family's church, which was a small

Spanish church. I presented my ministry in Spanish, and the church agreed to send a check over to the mission board to be placed in my account. I then presented at larger English-speaking churches the following Sunday. Sarah came with me not only for support but also to play the piano as I was given the opportunity to sing to help gain support. I sang "To Behold Thee" by Dan Forrest and "Do Not I Love Thee" by Phillip Doddridge and Craig Curry. I had both of these impressive songs in my repertoire because of their wide vocal range of hitting A-flats, which for reference is what the phantom sings in "Music of the Night" in Andrew Lloyd Webber's *The Phantom of the Opera*. I was happy to hear that both churches agreed to support me. Through the help of church support, money was provided for me to return to Peru. I taught for another year and continued my ministry there.

Sarah and I continued our friendship throughout the year, and I grew to love her, but as a friend. I knew that what I had going on inside of me wasn't going to magically disappear because I was dating a woman. If this was sound logic, then I would have seen evidence of this in my prior relationships. And while it may even have been fun to date her, I couldn't have her pay the price for that facade.

One night we were practicing music as we usually did. She played the piano, and I sang. That night, I remember singing "Take Me as I Am" from the musical *Little Women*. After the song, I sparked up a conversation about our relationship. I told her that I valued what we had, but I didn't want to lead her on if she was thinking about a relationship beyond being friends. I didn't go into detail about why, but I told her that I preferred to keep things platonic. She kindly respected the decision, and our friendship remained strong. We kept singing and playing piano and hanging out with the wonderful group of people from Musa.

I only saw Daniel at the church a few times after the first time I went there. Among those few times, I went out of my way to talk to him. He was about my age, a little shorter than me, and had a well-trimmed thin beard. He was always well-dressed and often wore a white baseball cap that contrasted his light-brown skin. He was one of the few who owned a car. I don't recall the model or make, but I remember how new and clean it was. And one afternoon he drove me around Lima as we made small talk about life in Lima, my hobby of music, and his of sports. We were clearly opposites and found little in common. I don't know why he agreed to hang out that afternoon, but I enjoyed looking at his beautiful face. I imagined what it might have been like to kiss him.

I grew very fond of Peru. I enjoyed living there and adopting the Peruvian culture and way of life. But there was still something missing. My heart ached for reprieve. I wanted rest from hiding. I taught and sang about God every day; I served faithfully in the local church, and I did my best to live righteously, but God felt like a million miles away. There was a void even the Omnipresent didn't fill.

Chapter Fourteen

You may be asking yourself why on earth I went to Peru as a missionary if I had such deep struggles with my sexuality and my faith. One of the main reasons I went to Peru was because I was determined to become godlier so that I would become less of a homosexual. I thought that if I became a missionary, then that would surely be enough to save me from such a heinous lifestyle. After all, missionaries were the pinnacle of the Christian life. We placed missionaries on pedestals. I looked at missionaries as if they were celebrities because they were giving their actual lives as a sacrifice for the ministry of Christ. They were the goal. How could you be a missionary and not find favor in the eyes of God?

I went to Peru and did all the right things. But guess what? Nothing changed. As a matter of fact, my desire for men actually grew as I was there. I'd become an expert at playing the good Christian guy. I was a missionary and involved in my church. I was teaching Bible classes and showing others what it meant to live a godly life. But I wasn't practicing what I preached. Not because I didn't want to, but because I was confused and tormented by the war going on within me. The more I tried to run from it, the stronger it became.

Many nights I would find myself in the midst of temptation. And the battle went something like this: *Should I pick up my phone and watch porn, or should I not?* I clashed with the right and wrong. I picked up my phone and looked at it. I then went further by scrolling to a specific app I had—but I didn't open it.

Fulfilling desires is normal. It can even be healthy. And I can always ask for forgiveness. No. I shouldn't. I then put my phone down, said a desperate prayer, and moved on to something else. I walked out of the room to focus my mind on anything but social media. But the thought remained tucked in the recesses of my mind. The yearning followed me to the next room, and I felt a tingle through my body. I would pick up a book, hoping to distract myself and get my mind off the temptation. But my thoughts returned to the images waiting on the screen, imagining what it would be like and how it would feel. I suddenly returned to the room with my phone, opened the app, and succumbed to the fiery desire within me.

Afterward, I immediately felt a numbing amount shame. I felt dirty. I hated myself. I felt so defeated that I questioned the validity of my faith as a whole. *How can I even be a believer and yet fall into this same sin time after time after time? A real Christian wouldn't keep sinning like this.*

I never felt good enough. And I cried out to God in agony for what I'd done. I felt confused that I still sinned even though I tried so hard not to. Was God even there? Why was He not helping me when I so clearly wanted His aid? I begged for understanding. But all I heard was deafening silence. Have you ever found yourself there? Have you ever prayed to God but felt like you were screaming into a void?

I felt like I could never win. I tried so hard my entire life to be a good person and to do the right thing. I ached to be a good Christian. I prayed until my knees were sore. I wept until my eyes burned. I cried out helplessly until my voice was hoarse. Nothing changed. I'd never felt so alone. I'd never felt like my faith was weaker. I could never measure up to the standard that had been set before me. I always failed because, at the end of the day, that thing that I was taught to hate lived within me.

I was disgusting. I was that person pastors preached against. I was the abomination. I was that nasty thing. And nothing I did changed that. I was scared. I was frustrated. I remember saying over and over again that I wasn't a homosexual. *I'm not a homosexual.*

I tugged at my hair in anguish as I cried out to God for mercy. I tried to read the Bible on a daily basis, but it felt like empty words entering my mind and leaving my thoughts before I could grasp them. I kept hearing about how other people felt like they had heard from God or that they had learned so much in their daily devotions.

Hearing this positive feedback made me wonder why I wasn't benefiting as much from my devotions. Was there something wrong with me? Of course, there was. I was gay, remember. God wasn't going to talk to me. I was taught that God only revealed His Word to those who knew Him, or rather, His children. I tried so hard to read and learn from the Bible, but it never made sense to me. It never clicked. Something had to change.

After trying my whole life to be the exemplary Christian everyone wanted me to be, I could no longer do it. The split lifestyle was too exhausting. My quest to rid myself of homosexuality by following God's path yielded no fruitful outcome. I'd given my whole life to God, doing God's work, and it still brought me no joy, and it certainly didn't help with my same-sex attraction.

I stood in the living room of my apartment in Peru and decided that enough was enough. I was gay. And I was finally ready to accept that. I admitted it to myself; and that was the first step.

This revelatory experience came about the time the second school year was ending. I was asked to extend another year, but I knew in my heart that my time in Peru had come to an end. If, after all this Christian work, I still found no relief from this spiritual game of tug of war, then something had to change.

My exit from Peru was bittersweet. I would miss the incredible people I'd come to know; I would miss the simple lifestyle I'd come to love; and I would miss the students. It was fulfilling watching them grow and learn. But it was time for me to go.

The lessons I learned in Peru are invaluable. I learned to slow down and appreciate the smaller things in life. When I was there, I focused on doing well in my job and developing healthy, long-lasting relationships. I invested in people, and it was a worthwhile investment.

Coming out to myself was necessary and difficult. It felt like I was choosing my homosexuality over God. Maybe that's the way it had to be. All my life, I had been sheltered in a pristine bubble. I had no understanding of the world or the people living in it. Looking at the world from within the safety of my bubble seemed enticing and fun, but living in it. . . well, I almost didn't survive.

PART
Three

Chapter Fifteen

I left Peru in the summer of 2015. I was twenty-five years old. I had no direction in life, so I moved back in with my parents who were living in Virginia. Once again, I went back to the drawing board to figure out my next steps.

Even though I'd come out to myself, I was still living an outward lie. I wasn't ready to come out to my family because I really didn't know what that meant, and I was relying on them for everything at that time. I didn't want to make things awkward, and I certainly didn't want to face the possibility of getting kicked out, if it came to that. So I acted like the pious Christian everyone was proud of while I determined my next steps.

Since I enjoyed to travel, I researched flight attendant jobs. I applied to United, American, and Delta. I was rejected by all three. I continued to apply to airlines until I finally received an interview from a small carrier, Trans States Airlines. I got up early the morning of the interview and drove an hour and fifteen minutes to the hotel just outside of DC where the interview was held.

There were about fifty candidates present; we all gathered in a big room for a presentation before the interviews started. We watched a short video about the company, and then a recruiter completed a presentation to get us excited about the job and the great benefits they offered.

After this presentation, we split up into groups and began interviewing. There were several recruiters conducting interviews, which was efficient. It didn't take long until I was called for my individual meeting. Afterward, I was thanked for my time and told that I would hear from them soon. After several days, I received a congratulatory email, inviting me to attend an eight-week flight attending training program in Missouri. I had a job and I was elated! I told my parents, and they congratulated me. I believe they were skeptical about my joining the secular world, especially the airline industry, but they supported my new adventure.

My mom drove me to the airport to catch an early morning flight from Washington, DC, to St. Louis, Missouri. I was nervous about this big change, and I knew my mom was worried about my well-being and this introduction into the "real" world.

On the drive, she said, "Jordan, your dad and I have tried to shelter you kids from the harshness of the world. There is going to be a lot of temptation where you're going, but I hope that you choose to glorify God with your decisions."

"I know," I responded. "I'll honor God and won't forget." I kept my focus on the road.

I was twenty-five years old and this was my first secular job. And the first time I would step out of the safe confines of the Christian bubble my parents had so carefully provided for me. As we arrived at the terminal, my mom said a reluctant goodbye. And I set out on my new adventure, unsure of what to expect.

The flight attendant training schedule was Monday through Friday, eight hours a day of both didactic and hands-on learning. We learned about the company, aviation, customer service, and safety within those eight weeks. We also spent a lot of time on the aircraft acting out scenarios by role-playing. We had exams each week, which had a minimum passing score. We also had to learn and perform safety drills as well as demonstrate exhaustive understanding of the safety equipment onboard the aircraft. Failure of these verbal or written exams resulted in dismissal from training. I studied a lot and made nearly perfect scores on all of the exams.

During training, I was still too nervous to come out to everyone. So I acted as straight as I could. At the time, I didn't realize that most of the men in the airline industry were gay, so I think it was probably assumed that I was gay. I remember one night I was studying with my friend and classmate, Gigi. With papers on her lap and an Oreo in her mouth, she asked, "So, are you gay?"

I looked at her with wide eyes as my mind raced for an answer. *Should I come out? Or should I not?*

"No, I'm not," I muttered.

She gave me a dubious look and said, "It's OK if you are. I was just wondering."

"Gotcha, well, I'm not gay. I definitely like women," I reiterated, and we went back to studying something about fighting fires if such an event occurred on the aircraft. Awhile later, I ran into Gigi on a layover in Houston and we had dinner together. I finally told her I was gay to which she replied, "I know." And we shared a few laughs and hugs.

The best part about flight attendant training was some of the people I met there. One such person was Jema Stubblefield. Jema had beautiful brown skin, thick black hair, and a smile that went from ear to ear. She was in her early twenties and from the DC area like me. She sat next to me during one of our first classes. She leaned over to me and asked if she could borrow a pen. I looked at her and whispered, "I was going to ask you the same thing." We both snickered under our breath. I knew from that moment that we would probably get along. Jema and I hung out together throughout training. We studied and went out together while imagining our lives as flight attendants living in D.C. Graduation couldn't come soon enough.

Graduating from flight attendant training was an exciting accomplishment for me. I couldn't wait to move to DC and fly around the country, serving passengers in the air.

My first trip was the standard three day of flying to and from different cities and staying in hotels overnight. On this first trip, I was accompanied by another flight attendant who helped train me and acclimated me to flying and the job duties. I was so excited for my first flight I could barely keep my feet on the ground. I walked with such pride through the airport as I made my way to the gate. I met the lady who was training me at the gate and she greeted me with a kind but stern welcome. We boarded the plane together.

I will never forget that first trip. My trainer enjoyed micromanaging. During the beverage service, as I was pouring beverages, she would instruct me on how I should be pouring. I thought that there was only one way to pour coffee into a paper cup, but apparently, there is a correct way. She would examine me as I was pouring and say, "No, too much," or "No, too little." She judged everything I did. Perhaps my greeting to the passengers wasn't friendly enough or maybe it was too friendly. The way I gathered trash in the cabin didn't live up to her standard, so I tried to be more graceful as I gently dropped the dirty cups and wadded up napkins in a gray, heavy-duty plastic trash bag as I gave a smile and said, "Thank you so much," to each passenger.

On the second night at the hotel, she and I sat down for a debrief in the lobby. She dug through her bag for a stack of papers that she slapped on the table as if trying to intimidate me. She looked at me, clicked her pen, and started to read through the papers out loud about my performance. She gave me a cold and calculating look, telling me that some people don't pass and have to repeat this portion of the flight training. I honestly thought she was going to fail me, and I would have to do the process over again.

She went through the checklists and made marks with her red pen. It seemed like it took forever to get through that meeting. Finally, she said that she would pass me. As soon as she dismissed me, I headed straight for my room as fast as I could and locked the door behind me.

I couldn't wait for this trip to be over. Being a flight attendant is important work, but it's not rocket science. It isn't a hard job. But this individual made it seem like it could only be done one way or else the whole system failed. Sorry, sis, but pouring coffee is not an art.

When we arrived back in DC, I didn't bother to say goodbye. I headed straight for the door to the parking lot, got in my car, and zipped home. As I was driving home, I burst into tears. What had just happened? What had I done? Most importantly, what was I going to do?

When I got home, I made a call to my manager to talk with her about what had just happened on the trip. I told her in detail about my experience. She reassured me that not every flight would be like what I'd experienced and that flying would get better. She encouraged me to keep moving forward. I took her advice, and flights did get better.

When I wasn't working, I spent a lot of time watching Netflix or listening to music in my room that I rented. When I needed a change in scenery I would camp out at the Dunkin' Donuts down the street for a few hours with a good book and a cup of coffee with cream and sugar. I spent a lot of time reading there. I read two books that I remember, *Jane Eyre* and *To Kill a Mockingbird*. I enjoyed reading because it allowed me to escape my reality for a while. Reading took the therapeutic place of singing since I didn't have much opportunity for music at the time.

Jema and I stayed in contact after flight attendant training. Our schedules were sporadic, so hanging out always proved to be a challenge. However, we did make it work as often as possible. The first time we hung out after training, Jema invited me to a bar in Manassas where she knew the bartender. I eagerly said yes, got in my car, and drove the thirty minutes from Chantilly to Manassas. When I arrived, we shared a big hug and ordered cosmopolitans. We swapped stories about our first few flights and acclimating to this new lifestyle. She then started to tell me about this guy she was dating. I wanted to come out to her, but I wasn't sure what to say.

As she was telling me all the details about this new guy, I kept rehearsing in my head what I might say if I did come out. Jema created a safe space with her kindness, and the way she talked about politics and acceptance of all people made me realize how progressive she was in her thinking. But even with people like her, the thought of coming out gave me butterflies in my stomach. I ordered another cosmopolitan to help build up some courage. We chatted a bit more about her man friend and then she asked me that dreaded question: "So, are you seeing anyone?"

This was my chance.

"Well, I have something to tell you." There was a short pause, and then I continued, "And that's that I'm gay."

She tilted her head to the side and gave the biggest smile.

She put her hand on my arm and said, "Oh, I know. I was just waiting for you to tell me. I love you so much, and I'm glad we can finally both talk about the men in our lives when you find someone."

We shared a tender hug. After coming out, the butterflies went away, and I felt a wonderfully liberating effect that sent a ripple from the depths of my heart and on through my entire body. I couldn't help but smile as I drove home that night.

Little by little I became more confident with my sexuality. Telling Jema helped boost my confidence. Now, I felt ready to dive into the dating world.

Chapter Sixteen

Part of the purpose of my move to DC was to find myself. I wanted to explore my sexuality. I'd lived under the strict rules of the Christian religion my entire life; now, I wanted to step into another world of discovery.

To start my pursuit, I downloaded dating apps I'd heard about during flight attendant training. I made profiles for all of them—Tinder, Grindr, Bumble, and so on, but I had no idea what I was getting myself into. As I joined this swiping game, I initiated the process of training my mind to judge people by their photos. It became rather addicting because I wanted to see how many people were swiping right on me and how many matches I could get. As I started swiping, I remember the moment I got my first match. The notification sounded, and the word *Matched* appeared across the screen in big green letters.

My heart jumped with surprise. *Wow! I matched. What do I do? Should I message them?* But I was always told to never talk to strangers on the internet. Putting my inhibitions aside, I sent the message.

I entered the gay dating scene with a conservative Christian worldview. While I wanted to step out of my bubble, I couldn't help but take my belief system with me. I was very judgmental, and I didn't understand the lifestyles of the people I started to meet. Through my formative years, I had been taught to look at the people in the world as sinners. They were lost, rebellious people who needed Jesus. We often preached at them and warned them about upcoming judgment if they didn't repent from their sinful ways. But we never took the time to understand them.

I remember one guy I started to hang out with was going through some deep personal and family struggles. He began to open up to me about a few issues he was having, so my initial reaction was to throw Bible verses at him, but I knew that wouldn't be received well. So I let him talk. He told me that he was going to therapy and that it was helping. When I heard that, he suddenly became unattractive to me. *Therapy* was a dirty word where I came from. People went to therapy because they were searching for answers in the wrong places. Mental health issues were a result of sinfulness and living a life apart from Christ.

I was always taught that Christians shouldn't be depressed because they have the peace and power of Christ within them. If one needed additional help, then they were to go to biblical counseling to help sort out their issues.

I questioned my friend's motives for going to therapy and voiced my disapproval. He was rightfully offended. I have since apologized for my ignorance and applauded him for taking the steps to go to therapy for help. Therapy is a very important aspect to healthy living and an excellent first step. Everyone should consider it from time to time.

Another guy I met through an app caught my attention, so we decided to meet up one evening; he suggested a restaurant that turned out to be rather fancy. Fancy restaurants were not familiar to me as my version of an upscale eatery was going out to the Olive Garden on a Saturday night. I felt a bit out of place. As I read the menu, I barely understood what I was seeing, but I was too embarrassed to ask. So I ended ordering something called *tartare* as it had the word *steak* in the description. I knew I liked steak, so I knew it couldn't be bad.

The server brought out a small plate with what looked like a round mold of raw beef. They set it in front of me, set my friend's order in front of him, and asked if there was anything else they could get us. I kindly said no and stared quizzically at the rare food I'd ordered. And rare it was indeed.

Between bites of trying to swallow this odd dish being careful not to chew too much, the conversation between my date and me was rather awkward. He complimented me often, and I didn't know how to react from a guy making verbal passes at me. I became easily embarrassed but kindly thanked him for his flattery. Then I would stare back down at my food and prepare for another bite of this cold, unfamiliar taste.

To fill the silence and to keep him from complimenting me further, I asked him about his job, his life, his likes and dislikes. I tried hard to find things in common, but it proved to be rather difficult. We didn't have much in common besides perhaps both wanting that dinner to end. When the check came, I made a silent gasp. My half cost almost a hundred dollars with tip. Mind you, I was only making fifteen dollars an hour at the time, and I spent almost a hundred dollars on a tiny portion of food that was too fancy for my simple palate.

As we prepared to leave, he told me that he was going to go see some friends who lived down the street. I politely declined the invitation and found my way back home thinking about the money and time I'd wasted with this person. Needless to say, we didn't go out again.

Before long, I matched with another guy with whom I began a conversation. He lived in DC and invited me to a bar in town. I accepted the invitation. When I arrived, we shared a quick greeting and made our way to the front to order drinks. Our chatting quickly turned into flirting as we ordered a few more drinks. With each drink, I became a little less tense and more talkative. We inched our chairs closer together and shared playful touches. We talked a bit more and then made our way back to the train.

As we waited for the train to come, we stood facing each other. He leaned in for a kiss. The moment our lips touched, an electric impulse shot through my body. This was the first time I'd kissed a guy, and it sent a tingle down my spine. We kissed again and again as I fully engaged in this make-out session. I oddly wasn't worried about the people around us and what they thought. I was completely mesmerized by the man in front of me and the fact that I was kissing him down in the hollow tunnels of the DC Metro.

When the train approached, we both boarded. I sat down, and then he sat next to me, putting his arm around me. We kissed several more times in between looking deep into each other's eyes as he told me how handsome I was. Then I would reply with, "Me? No, you!" And we'd kiss again. His stop was a few before mine. As we approached, we said good night, shared another kiss, and then he exited the train.

For me, the moment was magical. That night as I rode the train home, all I could do was smile and think about the magical kiss I'd had. When I arrived at my stop, I called Jema and gave her all the juicy details of the night I'd just had. She listened with anticipation as I shared my thoughts and feelings with her. This was the first time I'd ever done anything like this. And I let the moment live on in my head and treasured that fantasy in my heart. That was the first and last time I saw him.

One of the best perks about working for an airline is the flight benefits. Employees are able to fly anywhere in the United States for free or internationally and only pay the taxes. We had been given the gift of travel, and it was a gift indeed! During one of my breaks, I decided to fly to Chicago from DC for a couple of days. A good family friend, Angel, lived in Chicago. So I called her, and she hosted me for the weekend. At that time, I knew I wanted to live there some day.

When I arrived, Angel picked me up from the O'Hare airport, and we drove to her apartment in Lincoln Park. When we got there, she gave me the code to the elevator and a key to her door. She showed me to the room I would be staying in, and I got settled. I immediately started swiping through Tinder and matched with a few people. I messaged one guy who agreed to meet me out in town later that night. He took me to my first gay club in Chicago, Roscoe's.

We met at the club, shared an awkward first hug, and he said, "So, do you want to get drunk?"

I replied, "Yep!"

And so the night began.

It was a Friday night; the club was busy with people dancing, grinding on each other, and drinking regrettable amounts. That night, there was a special on pitchers of Long Island iced tea for thirteen dollars. I threw one back as we made our way to the dance floor. We danced without a care in the world, pressing up against the other people who filled the bar.

We ordered two more pitchers, allowing the alcohol to lower our inhibitions before we started to make out with each other and a few other random guys in the club. It felt good to hang on his lips and be in a crowd of people who were like-minded.

As we got deeper into the night, I could feel the alcohol catching up to me. I had that moment where I knew the night was over. It was late December in Chicago, so the temperature was freezing outside, but the alcohol acted as an insulator. I walked about a mile to get back to Angel's place. When I arrived, I went up the elevator and into her apartment. I immediately ran to the toilet just as I started to violently vomit.

I slept in late the next day, feeling incredibly hungover. I regretted my drinking choices from the night before. Angel asked me where I'd ended up going. Out of fear, I lied and told her that I went to a sports bar down the street. I don't know why I didn't want to tell her. She was like family to me and maybe I was afraid that if I told her, then she would be disappointed in me. A negative response from her was highly unlikely, but the familial relationship had been broken before and I didn't want to risk it again. I think she knew I was lying to her, but she let me come out to her in my own time. And when I did, she became a big supporter.

During that trip, I developed a connection with Chicago; It was a welcoming, exciting place, and I knew that I would be back. I just didn't know when or how.

Chapter Seventeen

Working for the regional carrier was often used as a stepping stone to get hired at mainline airlines like United and American. I wanted to work for a larger airline because they would offer better pay and better destinations. So I applied to United Airlines. When I received the invitation to interview in Newark, I was so excited that I could barely keep from jumping up and down. I prepped for the interview, pressed my suit, and made reservations at a hotel near where I would be interviewing.

The interview day was long but well-planned. I had a one-on-one interview with a recruiter and then moved through the different phases of the interview process. About four hours later, I was in the last phase and received a job offer. I accepted the invitation to flight attendant training that would start in a few weeks in mid-January.

Even though I'd accepted the invitation, there was still something within me that didn't feel right. You know when you want to do something in your mind, but your heart is telling you something else? I had that feeling. Would life really better at this company? Could I make enough money to live in a big city like San Francisco? I say San Francisco because that's what they were advertising. Perhaps it was time to start nursing school.

I knew, though, that it was time to resign from my current position. The following day, I went to my manager and gave her my formal resignation. Since I'd quit my job in DC, I moved back in with my parents until I decided what I wanted to do. I had some time to deliberate since training wasn't for another couple of weeks.

When I moved back into my parents' place, I had to readjust to a conservative lifestyle. While there, I was expected to attend church and live a life that appeared to be honoring and glorifying to God. In a way, I had to go back in the closet.

My parents had built a house on the top of a mountain at the end of a dirt road. The closest grocery store was twenty minutes away, and my parent's house had an assortment of deer, turkeys, and even black bear sometimes as neighbors. I'd always been a city boy at heart. I liked the business of the streets and the easy access to coffee shops and stores. Secluded country living wasn't for me.

The following days, I analyzed my future until I drew out every possible scenario detailing the good, the bad, and the ugly of all of them. But I still couldn't settle on a decision. I thought about playing it safe by going to nursing school. But it would take two years for me to get my associates degree in nursing, which seemed like an eternity. Could I live with my parents on top of that mountain for two years? Could I go back in the closet for two more years? Or I could move to a big city as a flight attendant, experience the unknown, and continue to live out my gay fantasy.

I still had a decision to make, and time was running out. My training class was set for January 26, 2016. On January 25, I sent an email to one of the representatives at United and informed them that I wouldn't be attending training due to "personal reasons." I wasn't even sure what those reasons were, but I made the decision, and as soon as I hit the send button, I felt a deep void in my stomach. I sealed my place on top of that mountain.

The following days I began to feel incredibly isolated. I was twenty-five years old, living with my parents. I didn't have a job. I barely had money in the bank, my friends were far away, and I was at the starting point of a sexual identity crisis in an unforgiving environment. I'd just given up what I thought was my dream job, and I had nothing to show for it. I knew that the alternative was nursing school, but the end goal seemed so out of reach that I couldn't visualize it. I fell into this depressive trance where I spent a lot of time in my room waiting for the time to pass by watching the TV show *Friends* on Netflix or endlessly scrolling through Facebook. I felt trapped by my own reality because I wasn't moving forward. I was moving backward into a very dark corner.

Chapter Eighteen

I remember one evening my mom came to my room and finally asked me what was going on—I seemed upset all the time. Without saying a word, I burst into tears. And I couldn't stop. I was overwhelmed, but I couldn't talk about why because I was afraid. I knew how my parents would react. And I wasn't strong enough to have that fight. I also knew I couldn't keep my secret in for much longer.

Between the sobs, I told her that I wished our relationship were better. But I couldn't have a good relationship with someone who wouldn't accept me for who I was. I ached to be accepted. I wanted to be understood. But there is no acceptance and understanding where there's disagreement. My mom gave me a silent hug and told me that her life before she was saved was miserable. She said that she didn't want that experience for her or her children. She continued with tenderness by saying that the choices we make are our prerogative, but choices that are dishonoring to God won't be tolerated in their house. She gave me a nod and walked out of my room.

One night at dinner, I'd made it up in my mind that I would come out to my parents and take whatever it was that was coming my way. I remember my mom made a delicious squash soup with a side salad and homemade sourdough bread. I looked out the window while I sat at the kitchen table and saw the sun setting over the Shenandoah mountains. Hues of purple and pink filtered the blue sky as the deep orange sun tucked itself behind the strong mountain range.

I wish my coming out could be as beautiful as that, I thought. But I prepared myself for just the opposite.

My dad took a seat at the head of the table to my right, and my mom was tossing a salad in the kitchen. The local Christian music station was playing softly in the background. My mom brought the salad over and sat down as my dad said a prayer for the food. We made light conversation, and I mentioned that I wanted to talk about something. As I struggled to articulate what I wanted to say, my mom interjected and took the words out of my mouth.

She looked at me with an expression of apprehension, disgust, and fear as she posed the formidable question, "Jordan, are you a… homosexual?"

I locked eyes with her for a few seconds as the song "Praise You in This Storm" filled the silence; my brain raced to comprehend what had just happened as I decided what to do in that moment.

I said in a matter-of-fact tone, "Okay, so this is how we're doing it? Then, yes. Yes, I am."

My answer initiated a long debate between my parents and me about my sexual identity. Tension grew and the mood of the room took on a mixture of sadness, depression, disappointment, and questioning.

I told my parents that my being gay wasn't a choice; rather, I was born with a natural sexual attraction toward men. I explained to my mom that I looked at men the way she looked at men. I explained that she didn't choose to be straight just like I didn't choose to be gay. In fact, if I did have the choice, then I would have chosen to be straight. I wouldn't wish this upon anyone.

While my parents listened to my arguments, they were firm in their faith and leaned on their interpretation of what the Bible said about homosexuality. My parents pleaded with me to go to biblical counseling to change my ways, but I kindly declined their request. My dad told me that he felt like they had failed as parents. And at that moment, I felt like I'd failed as their child. To say that I felt broken would be an understatement.

I ultimately told my parents that I was who I was, and that I wouldn't change. I reiterated to them that I couldn't fight it anymore.

My mom looked at me from across the table and said, "Jordan, son, if you choose this lifestyle, then you will be living in blatant disobedience to God."

"Well, so be it, then. This misery has to end at some point," I said.

"You will never be happy without God," my dad interjected.

"I wasn't happy with him either," I rebutted. "For my whole life, I tried to be the model Christian. I went to Christian school. I was involved in church. I didn't do drugs or drink alcohol like some of the other kids. I went to Bible school (twice). I even went to Peru as a missionary to try to find God, but nothing worked. My heart wasn't fulfilled, and joy wasn't found.

"God didn't meet me where I was. He wasn't there when I tried to find Him. I begged him for help. I pleaded until my knees were raw that he would rescue me. But he didn't. I tried every way possible to do the right thing, but where has it got me? So I'm done fighting for Him. I'm done sacrificing myself for the Gospel in hopes that one day I'll finally be set free of my misery. The only thing I haven't tried is my own way—accepting that I am who I am. I finally accept myself as being gay, and I'm OK with that. I wish you would be, too," I said in a resolute tone.

With a sternness, my mom wrote the law. "If that's what you're doing, then listen closely. No men will be coming to this house. You will not be out late, and you will not be drinking. If I find alcohol in your room or in this house, then you're out. Do you understand?"

I gave a sideways glance, and the conversation ended. The narrative stopped there. A wall was built—one that I'd begun years ago. A fortress, stronger than ever, was constructed with the exchange I'd just had with my parents. Everything was now out in the open. It was them against me. And I'd died inside.

The first bombshell hit, disrupting our lives and causing burdens to be carried on behalf of my parents and me. My parents were blindsided by the news and believed that my decision to accept being gay was in direct violation of God's law, the Bible. It shook their faith because they didn't want to see their child hurting but they also could not in good faith accept what they believed to be wrong. It was a tough spot to be in. For me, the news of coming out backfired in my face even though I knew what to expect. The real thing was worse. I wanted to be accepted, but I felt like an outcast. I wore a scarlet letter, and it broke me.

At that time, I'd hit an all-time low. I'd arrived at rock bottom. I could barely get out of bed. I spent hours staring at the wall, begging for the time to pass. I felt completely helpless. I'd never been so lost before in my life. Between the episodes of lying motionless on the floor and enviously scrolling through Instagram, I looked for jobs and sent out my resume. Jobs in the area were slim, but I knew I had to do something. I knew that I couldn't spend the rest of my days cooped up in my room.

I must have sent out fifty resumes. As I waited to hear back, I spent my time watching Netflix and drinking wine I'd snuck into the house out of defiance. I preferred white wine, but I drank a red because it didn't have to be chilled. I hid it in a suitcase under some clothes. A dresser was in the room, but I lived out of the suitcase because it gave me hope that one day I would leave.

At night, after my parents went to bed, I popped the cork and poured a few glasses as I watched reruns of *Friends*. I found comfort in the glass of wine as it slowly calmed my nerves and made me feel OK for once. I made this a nightly routine. Occasionally, I would do a face mask as I sipped on my five-dollar bottle of pinot noir. I grew up in a family where men don't do face masks, so doing one felt highly liberating for me. It was a small step toward accepting who I was and allowing myself to enjoy being me, even if it was in the dark.

Since I'd declined the invitation for flight attendant training, I wasn't able to reapply for six months. So, I decided to focus my time on applying to nursing school. I needed to complete a few prerequisite courses before entering the nursing program at the local community college, so I began looking at options for taking online courses.

I signed up for my first class—a nutrition class. I wasn't particularly interested in the subject, but it gave me something to do. I poured all of my time and effort into that class. Almost every day, I would get in my car and drive thirty minutes to the closest Starbucks in Winchester where I would camp out for most of the day. I made the effort because I wanted to feel like I was a part of something. I had to get out of the woods and back into the city. With all the resumes I had sent out, I hoped that at least one would catch the attention of someone. And it did, but it wasn't a job I'd expected.

Chapter Nineteen

One afternoon, I received a phone call from a manager at a local bank. Her name was Kim. She was very kind and made our conversation very easy and comfortable. I had zero banking experience and no knowledge of business, and I was absolutely terrible with money. But I was willing to learn. Kim told me that she was looking to hire someone who could learn the banking process and then eventually start teaching classes to new hires. I had a background in teaching, so I used that experience to fluff my answers. She said that she was impressed and wanted to bring me in for an in-person interview. We picked a time, and I went in to the bank. While I didn't give stellar answers, Kim and I connected well.

A few hours after I got home, Kim called me and extended a job offer. I accepted over the phone and would start the following Monday, a week away. I was honest with Kim, and told her that I would like to transfer to the Fairfax branch (near DC) as soon as I was able to. Luckily, my transfer wouldn't be a problem, and I could still do the teaching from there. It would be at least six months or more before my transfer. And I immediately began counting down the days.

My new job would be Monday through Friday from 8:00 a.m. to 4:00 p.m. with alternating weekends. I quickly found out that banking wasn't my forte. My coworkers were nice, but the minutes felt like hours. I didn't understand banking. And it turned out that being a teller wasn't that interesting. Every day I arrived at work and thought about my transfer to Fairfax. I kept on saying to myself, "One day. One day I will get back there, but I have to get through this part first."

Living with my parents during this time was uncomfortable. While we didn't share many interactions, there was still mutual love and respect. I told my parents that I preferred not to go to church. Though they were disappointed, they didn't force me to go. It was a surprising win for me, and I needed to take back some control of my life.

When I would get home from work around five, I'd eat a quick meal with my parents at their house or sometimes we would go across the street where my brother lived with his wife and two young kids. Besides the occasional dinner, I didn't spend much time there. I preferred to be alone in my room rather than with people who I had to hide myself from. Neither my parents nor I shared the news of my coming out with my siblings. My parents agreed that it was my decision to tell them when and if I wanted to. I didn't come out to them because I didn't have the strength to keep having the same discussions with people who didn't understand what I was going through. To them the choice was simple and easy—choose God because being gay is a sin. But it's not that simple. There is nothing easy about not being able to love who you love. There is nothing easy about being an effeminate guy. There is nothing easy about questioning your sexual identity. It's not easy to restructure your brain to abide by social norms. I couldn't keep defending myself to my family, so I said nothing at all about the matter.

Though I was happy to have some funds coming in, I still carried around a tremendous burden. I couldn't be real with people or my family. There was no one like me around. I remember watching as business-women frequented the bank. They looked so chic in their pencil skirts and high-heeled pumps. They walked with confidence and had power.

I wish that could be me, I thought. The only realness I had were the scenes I made in my head.

Kim knew that I had a city flair and encouraged me to find a place of my own. But renting was expensive, and I needed to save for my transfer to Fairfax. She'd always say to me, "There's something about you that's different, but I can't put my finger on it." I would just smirk and think, *If you only knew.* Kim had a bright smile and a personality that brought a lot of laughter to the workplace. She was kind and had a warm presence that made you feel encouraged. Interacting with her was the highlight of my days there.

One night as I was scrolling through Facebook, I saw that one of my friends who I'd met at my previous airline had received a job offer at American Airlines. I reached out to congratulate him and ask him about his experience. He told me that they were still hiring and that I should apply.

I stopped my studies to work on my resume and submitted my application that night on February 7, 2016. On March 7, I received an email invitation for a video-recorded interview. My parents were at my brother's house across the street making dinner, so I chose that night to set up a small interview area in the living room. I sat in front of my computer and clicked on the first question. A flight attendant popped up on the screen and asked a question. A thirty-second timer began to count down, which allowed time for preparation, and there were three minutes to complete an answer.

During the video interview, there was no stopping or rerecording. I felt like I'd panicked through the whole process. I was sweating, and my heart kept pounding. I felt as if I'd bombed that interview. I took off my suit and tie, threw on some jeans, and walked across the street to join the others at dinner. My mind kept replaying all the questions and the answers I'd given. Though this time, I came up with better answers that I wish I'd used instead of the actual ones I did. I kicked myself for not thinking better on my feet.

The following days I refreshed my email a hundred times a day to see if I'd received anything from American. Finally, on March 20, I received an email from talent acquisition inviting me to do a face-to-face interview, which would take place on March 26. I couldn't believe what I was reading. The interview day was a Saturday, which happened to be the weekend that I didn't work. I was elated with the news.

The interview process was intense. All of the applicants started together in a large room. We were given fifteen minutes to mingle with one another before the official interview process began. From the moment we stepped into the room and found our seats, there were interviewers scattered throughout the room with small pads of paper, taking notes. They watched our every move and our every interaction with those around us. It felt like being under a microscope.

The next phase was a group interview. There were six people in my group. We sat in the front of the room with four interviewers sitting directly in front of us. One interviewer would ask a question and then allow us to answer in any order we wanted. For the last question, instead of getting the same question, we picked out a random question from a glass bowl and then answered it. The inquiry I pulled from the bowl read, "Who is your hero and why?"

My hero at that time was Martin Luther, the German priest and theologian, because of his courage and leadership. He stood up for what he believed in in the midst of great adversity and opposition. As I answered the question, I locked eyes with one of the interviewers who had a big, warm smile. We connected in that moment, and she made me feel comfortable.

As we made our way through the different phases of the interview, I noticed that fewer and fewer people were around. I figured it was a good thing that I was still there. As I sat in one of the rooms, my name was called. I was greeted by a man in a flight attendant uniform who sat in a chair across from the one I was sitting in. He posed a few basic questions that I answered confidently and enthusiastically. He then told me that he wanted me to read an announcement that would be done on the aircraft. I found it a bid odd, but I read with excitement.

As I neared the end of the speech, I read the words, "We would like to extend a conditional job offer and invite you to join one of our initial flight attendant training classes." I fumbled through those words, not knowing if it was real or if it was just a part of the announcement.

I looked over at the interviewer sitting across from me who had a big smile on his face as he said, "Congratulations!" He asked if I would like to accept the invitation to training, and I immediately said, "Yes." And this time, there was no doubt in my mind about accepting. I left nursing behind to embark on this new journey; most importantly, I used this job as a way to get out of Virginia.

I went into the bank on Monday and asked Kim if we could talk. I walked into her office and sat down. I felt awkward having this conversation after having just started working there not even two months earlier. I looked down at the floor and admitted to her that I was very unhappy.

She looked at me and said, "I know." I told her that an airline had offered me a job, and that I would be putting in my two weeks' notice. She accepted my resignation and wished me the most happiness. And I knew that it was genuine. Kim wanted me to be happy, and she was excited for my new beginnings. And so was I.

PART

Four

Chapter Twenty

I arrived at training both enthusiastic and nervous. I was eager for the friends I would make and the things I would learn about flying and customer service. I was amazed by how professional and clean everyone looked at the training center. The facility was immaculate, and the training devices were state of the art. Each aircraft from the MD-80 to the newest Boeing 787 Dreamliner had a real-life simulation trainer. We trained on the models as we went through various safety scenarios such as how to fight fires and to evacuate the aircraft in the event of an emergency.

Every simulation was lifelike, and the instructors made it fun. There were tests each week with a minimum passing score. Failed exams led to further instruction, and two consecutive fails resulted in dismissal from training. Training lasted six weeks of intense, hands-on learning. The pressure was high. But it was unforgettable. As I met my fellow classmates that first day, I felt a sense of ease. And I thought, *This is going to be good. I'm going to be all right.*

My roommate Jean Pierre (JP) and I immediately hit it off well. One of the first things we found in common was Peru, where he had been born and raised. That connection paved the way to a wonderful and strong relationship. We shared many laughs and late-night talks. He was just the kind of person I was looking for in my life at the time. He was older than I was and had been out for a while. In fact, he was in a long-term, committed relationship. He knew all the things I was wanting to know, and he served as a wonderful teacher to me in ways I'm sure he never even knew.

During the first couple of weeks of training, I developed quite the crush on a guy named J. J was two classes ahead of me, but we often passed each other in the halls or in the dining room. Or sometimes in the dormitories. The first time I noticed him, we were walking down the hall in opposite directions. We looked at each other as we passed by, and I got that tingle down my spine. He was tall and thin with broad shoulders, had green eyes, short, brown hair, and a beautiful smile that showed all of his perfectly white teeth. We saw each other a few times, and I remember thinking, *Well, hot diggity, who is that?*

A few days later, I got a notification on my phone from Grindr. I opened it, and it was him. The message read, "Hey! I think I've seen you around, and we've passed each other in the halls. My name is J. How are you?"

My heart leaped, and I started to compose a response, but then deleted it and rewrote it a few more times. I wanted him to know that I was interested and excited to hear from him, but also not so excited that I made it awkward.

"Hey! Yeah, I remember seeing you. I'm glad you messaged. My name is Jordan. It's nice to Grindr you, J."

We messaged back and forth a few times. I found out that he was from Puerto Rico but had moved to the States for college. He'd been living in Florida and working at Disney as a dancer for the last several years, but was looking for a career change and more stable finances.

"We will have to get together sometime soon. What floor are you on?" he asked.

"Yeah, I would like that. What about tomorrow after class? I'm on the second floor. What about you?" I replied.

"That's works. I'm on the third floor. Let's meet here tomorrow."

I couldn't wait for us to meet. That night I told JP about my new friend, J. He looked at me with a smirk. "Ooh, you got a boy toy already?" he asked in a playful tone as he chuckled.

"No," I said with a smile. "We are probably just going to hang out."

"Mmmm. Okay," JP muttered with a dubious look.

The next night, I met J at his room like we had planned the previous evening. He opened the door and happily invited me in. His roommate was gone for the night visiting family who lived in town, so we had the room to ourselves.

The room was similar to mine. As I walked in, there was a twin-size bed against the wall to the left, and to the right was a small sitting area with two chairs, a desk, and a minifridge with a few beers and half of a leftover sandwich. There was a small divider at the head of the twin bed to provide some privacy. Straight back, there was a queen bed to the left, and the bathroom was on the right. The decor was minimalist in style. I looked around and there were two giant suitcases that were used as dressers and clothing hung across the chair backs.

J had the queen bed and motioned me to come make myself comfortable. We talked for a while about training, and I picked his brain about what was to come as he was two classes ahead of me, which meant he was two weeks ahead. He then told me about his time at Disney and how much he loved dancing there. He showed me a barrage of photos that depicted a very exciting life he had there. The pictures showed him dancing in shows like *The Lion King* and *Cinderella*. One day he'd paint himself as if to blend in with an African tribe, and the next day he was looking dapper as a prince in a white suit.

After showing me a digital review of his life, he asked me about mine. I told him that I lived in Peru and worked for another airline before coming here. He was so excited to hear about my Peruvian adventures. And we engaged in a little bit of conversational Spanish.

J was kind and had a bubbly personality. I could tell through his photos and our time together that he was the life of the party. And he was good at making people feel good. I remember him just staring into my eyes and telling me how beautiful they were.

I blushed, turned away, and said, "Oh, you don't mean that."

"No, I really do," he said.

I looked at the time, and it was already past 10:00 p.m. I told him I should get going.

"Well, why don't you stay the night?" he said in a casual tone. He then laid back in bed and put his hands behind his head. "I'll be good. I promise."

I agreed to stay. I lay down next to him as he kept the side lamp on.

My heart began to accelerate as I lay there next to this incredibly handsome guy. I wanted to feel him but also wasn't going to make the first move. *Will he?* I wondered.

I then turned my head to look at him and he at me. We communicated with our eyes as we both inched a little bit closer. Then a little closer. I could feel my heart racing faster as the urge to touch his lips with mine grew stronger with every second. I felt a force pulling us closer like a magnet to metal.

We were so close I could smell the Chanel on his neck. We closed our eyes and gently locked our lips together. His lips were soft like satin, and his skin felt like that of a baby's.

He took off his shirt, revealing a perfectly chiseled six-pack. I went weak as I ran my hand down his chest and across his abdomen, feeling the ridges of his abs until I got to the waistband of his underwear.

We kissed over and over again as he reached over and turned off the lamp.

The next morning, I woke up early. J was still asleep, but I needed to get showered and ready for class. I gave him a light kiss on the forehead, threw on my clothes, and tiptoed out the door.

When I got back to my room, JP greeted me and said, "Aaaand where were you?"

I gave a big smile and said nonchalantly, "I was with J."

JP let out a laugh. "Uh-huh. And?"

I proceeded to tell JP every detail of this night. He listened intently and eagerly. I'd never been able to have this kind of talk with another gay man before. And this was exactly what I'd been looking for. I wasn't sure what would happen between J and me, but I was riding high on the previous night.

Training was very busy with classes and hands-on drills we practiced for evacuation purposes in the event of emergencies. But J and I made time to hang out. And we studied together. One evening I was helping him study by quizzing him on some of the safety features on the Boeing 777 he was studying. I told him for every answer he got right he would get a kiss. After a lot of right answers and a lot of kisses, he said in his thick Spanish accent, "I like this game!"

Another night we were studying together, and his mom called on Face-Time. He introduced me to her. He pulled me over so my face was visible in the screen, and he said, "This is my friend, Jordan!" as he moved his eyebrows up and down simultaneously as if to insinuate we were something more. "He speaks Spanish too!"

I thought, *Wow, he talks to his mom so openly about his guy friends. What must that be like?* I envied him because he had that type of relationship with his mom. And there was no judgment or disgusted looks. *I want that*, I thought. *I want that because I want an open and honest relationship where I don't have to hide or be someone who I'm not.*

During training, we were given the opportunity to choose where we would like to be based as flight attendants. While we were not guaranteed to get our first choice, that choice was often granted. All of the bases were open for our class, which included Dallas, Miami, Chicago, Boston, Los Angeles, and San Francisco. Chicago was my first choice. My dreams of living in Chicago and making it in a big city were coming to fruition. We submitted our choices, and a few days later our assignments were presented to us.

The instructors always made a big deal out of our base assignments. Everyone was so excited to know where they'd be going. So, with hip-hop music, flashing lights, and sparkling glow sticks, our bases would be revealed, and we all went crazy with excitement. I was handed an envelope with a piece of paper that resembled a plane ticket.

As I scoured the paper trying to make sense of what it meant, I found the destination, "ORD," which is the airport code for O'Hare Airport. I let out a huge sigh of relief and a shout of exuberance. In three weeks, I was headed for Chicago! I told J the news of my base assignment, and to my delight, he told me he was also headed to Chicago.

Throughout the next couple of weeks, I didn't see much of J like I had before. During every one of our breaks, I would get out my phone from my backpack, hoping to see a text from him, but there rarely was. I felt sad that we weren't communicating as much because I'd grown attached to him through our time spent together and the physical relationship we'd also engaged in. But why was he pulling back?

I brought this up to JP a few times. He told that I needed to relax. He said that I couldn't get too attached to people so quickly because there was no guarantee that they'd stick around, especially if they didn't express they wanted something more. He told me that I needed to learn to guard my heart and not fall for every guy who wanted to hook up with me. He said that it was important to establish boundaries early on when meeting someone so that no one got hurt, like I was.

What he said made sense and was something I hadn't thought about before. I was new to this, and I liked that handsome guys wanted to be with me. But that also meant that I needed to learn how to protect myself.

J and I sat down, and he told me that he wasn't looking for something serious right now. He needed to focus on graduating from training and starting his life in Chicago. He wanted to remain friends and told me that we could hang out once we got to Chicago. I understood and agreed that it was better to focus on the both of us graduating. We remained amicable but didn't have any more physical hangouts during training.

While I was excited about moving to Chicago, I only had three weeks to find a place to live. I immediately started looking for apartments. I posted on Facebook that I was moving to Chicago and asked if anyone knew about available apartments. One of my friends responded and put me in touch with someone who was looking for a roommate. The resident sent me pictures of the place and details about the rent. It was located in Logan Square right next to the Blue Line train station, which went straight to O'Hare. If that wasn't enough to convince me, then the rent ($575/month, utilities included) would be. I told him that I was interested.

As all of the new flight attendants entered our last week of training, we were eager to graduate and head to our new homes. One of the last parts of training included a simulation flight to one of our premium destinations. The flight took place on the Boeing 767 aircraft and included everything a real flight would have included, such as boarding, seating, and food. This was an opportunity for us to become familiar with what a passenger would experience on an international flight sitting in first class.

On a real international flight, the 767 would work eight flight attendants and one purser (lead flight attendant). Our instructors picked nine of us to act as the crew on this flight to London while the rest of the class were passengers in first class. As we sat in class, the instructors told us about this unique experience and informed us that they had chosen specific people for the crew. They called the aisle flight attendants forward. Then they called the flight attendant who would be working in the kitchen (galley), and then they finally called the lead flight attendant.

Before mentioning the name, they said that they'd taken great care in choosing this individual. They had been observing us for the last six weeks, and they wanted to use this opportunity to recognize and honor the hard work we had done and the character they saw. They built up the anticipation of who would play the lead and then finally announced who it would be. They said, "The purser on our flight to London will be Jordan Roberts!"

I thought I'd heard them incorrectly, but as they motioned me down, they assured me that they had indeed said my name. I couldn't believe it. What did they see in me? I didn't think I did anything special. I was humbled by the experience, and it's one I'll never forget.

Training opened me up to a world of acceptance and allowed me to be around like-minded people. It felt good not to have to hide and to be real with others. As training came to an end, I started to pack my things, say "see you soon" to the friends I had made and set my focus on moving to Chicago. It's finally happening.

Twenty One

I was finally where I wanted to be. I was free from the Christian bubble my parents had placed me in that had stripped me of my gay liberties. No more boundaries, no more people telling me no or that I shouldn't do something. All I had were the voices in my head warning me against sin, but it was my choice whether to listen to them. I chose to silence them. This was my time to live without reservation. I could finally let the gay out, and it felt good.

Living in the city offered progressive thinking and open-mindedness. There was room for everyone, as long as you wanted to join in. And I was ready to conform to their lifestyle.

I walked down the streets, noticing men in heels and makeup, pushing the boundaries of gender-identifying clothing. There were Pride flags outside of houses or businesses. People promoted acceptance, and differences were celebrated, all in the name of self-expression. I'd never existed in a place where it was OK to just be me. It felt like my liberation day, and I could finally breathe.

When I arrived in Chicago, I went to see the apartment I was interested in. I took the Blue Line train, which dropped me off at Logan Square. I walked down the street to the apartment building conveniently located near the train station along a road lined with large trees and strategically placed flowers. The current resident, Doug, invited me in to see the place.

I walked in to the smell of what seemed to be a high school locker room. The place was dirty, and it was apparent that it hadn't been cleaned in quite some time. The bathroom was small, and the tub had a yellow stain that lined the entire length of it. While I silently gagged,

I said that I liked the place and requested to see the application. I didn't have anywhere else to go, and I knew that I wouldn't be living there for forever. Furthermore, Doug was very nice and seemed to be a good roommate. The landlord, Jose, met me at the apartment that day and presented me the lease. I took the risk and signed it. Then I wrote a check for $575 and handed it to Jose.

The next day, I moved all my stuff in. And by all my stuff, I mean my two suitcases and one carry-on bag. I traveled light. At that time, I barely had two pennies to rub together, but I was happy to be there. I didn't even own a bed, so I went to Target and purchased an air mattress, which I slept on for the first six months. I was in the city of my dreams, working as a flight attendant and making a life for myself. I was slowly coming out of the mire I felt like I had been in.

My flying schedule was a bit unpredictable. Everything was based on seniority, meaning that, depending on how long you had been with the company, you had more control over your schedule and the trips you chose to fly. Since I was new, my choices were slim. Every other month, I was on call. This meant that I could be called at any time to work a trip, and I had to be at the airport within two hours. I usually had four to five on-call days a week.

I was ecstatic to begin my life in Chicago. City living is what I'd always wanted to do, and now here I was, living in one of the biggest and most beautiful cities in the United States. During those beginning days, I explored much of the city. I rode the Blue Line train into downtown on several occasions, walked the streets and sat in coffee shops as I read books I'd borrowed from the library. The library had eight floors and just about every book you could imagine. And they had music practice rooms with pianos. I signed up for free for a library card and immediately started using the practice rooms, bringing old sheet music I had from college. I practiced piano and sang like no one was listening. Doing music again filled my heart.

One of the first books I checked out of the library was a compilation of plays. Among them was one of my favorites, *The Man Who Came to Dinner* by George Kaufman and Moss Hart. I'd seen Dr. Maxwell (Alyssa's dad) direct this play when I was living in Pennsylvania, which had stuck with me all these years later. It is a comedy about a radio celebrity, Sheridan Whiteside, who accepts a dinner invitation by a local family in Ohio while on his tour. When he arrives at the house, he slips on a patch of ice and injures himself, forcing him to stay with the family for an extended period. The play is a comedic battle between this family and their new, demanding guest.

I took my new book through the streets of Chicago until I found a nice coffee shop to sit and read. Between the pages, I looked around as I sipped my latte noticing the business of the people around me. I loved the rhythm. Everyone had a place to go. The sound of the door opening and closing, construction workers working as the sound of metal on metal reverberated the streets. People talked on their phones over the melody of car horns on the busy streets outside. I sat back and smiled and thought, *This is great.*

Suddenly, my phone rang loudly, giving me a little bit of a startle. The caller ID read, "Euless Tx." That only meant one thing—work.

I answered the phone, "Hello?"

"Hello, Flight Attendant Roberts, this is Nick in crew scheduling. I have a trip for you."

"OK. What is it?" I replied.

"You'll be going to London tonight on the 787. You'll be position three. Your sign-in time is 1900."

"Wow, OK! Thanks," I replied.

I guess I was going to London tonight. Good thing I'd had that coffee. I packed up my things and headed straight home. I already had my suitcase packed, so all I needed to do was put on my uniform and head out the door.

Flying to London from Chicago was about a seven-and-a-half to eight-hour flight. We worked through the night, and once our service was through, we took our breaks in shifts. On this particular aircraft, there were bunk beds in the ceiling in the back of the plane.

When I arrived at the gate, I recognized one of the crewmembers—it was J. It was good to see him, work with him, and explore London with him. When we arrived in London, we checked in to our hotel, settled into our rooms, and took naps. The jet lag was difficult as London was six hours ahead of the United States. During that trip, we saw the London Bridge, Big Ben, and took our photo in one of the red phone booths. At one point, I remember using Wi-Fi to call my sister to brag about my time in London. She shared my excitement as I sat in a café and drank some tea, like a true British citizen. I still hadn't come out to her or my brothers. It still didn't feel like the appropriate time. They were all just excited about the flight benefits they now could take advantage of. And I was happy to share with them.

Not every time trip was glamorous like that one, but I was excited to be in my new job and in an exciting city. One of my favorite things to do was walk the Chicago river walk. There was something peaceful about walking along the winding river while looking up at the tall buildings that illuminated the sky above me. This was my city, and I loved it.

Somehow I thought that moving to Chicago would fix my problems. But the antagonizing existence of choosing between gay and God continued to weigh on me. When will the war end? It was time to make a choice.

Chapter Twenty Two

As I began navigating the gay world, I didn't know who I was; I had no idea where to even start. While I still holding on to my Christian worldview, I needed to explore who I was as a gay person. And this caused a tension that was in conflict with my spirit. I wanted to go all out in the gay scene, but something was holding me back because the essence of my spirituality was still very much alive in my mind. It wasn't easy to deconstruct a worldview when it was something I based truth in. Which meant, anything that went against it was a lie. But I worked to build new patterns of thinking which allowed acceptance of myself.

During my first month living in Chicago, I remember receiving a phone call from my brother-in-law. He and I had shared many deep conversations over the years and had become quite close, developing a mutual respect for one another. During that phone call, I came out to him and told him that I was choosing to accept myself as gay. I told him that I didn't know where I stood as far as Christianity or God, but I knew that it was time for me to be honest with myself about who I was sexually, and that it was time to stop hiding.

I told him that as I began to explore who I was as a gay person, I chose to forsake my fake identity in Christ. I'd tried for so many years to win the Christian battle, but the standard defeated me. I bowed out. I never felt judgment from him. He told me that it was OK to figure out who I was. He told me that my Christian background had failed me and that God was much more than a list of man-made rules.

I questioned God and His role in this world. How could a loving God allow such awful things to happen? I'd heard this question before when I was studying in college, and the answer was always rooted in faith. When there wasn't an answer, it was faith. I, however, wanted real answers. I wanted an explanation. How could God allow so much suffering? I saw people struggling through life doing the best they could do with what they had. I was always taught that people lived the way they did because of rebellion, but I saw that they were doing it because they had nothing else to help the pain they were experiencing.

As part of my journey to finding myself, I lost my moral compass. I found that the more photos I posted showing the most skin rewarded me the most attention. So I began to post more seductive photos on social media in hopes of getting more likes and more attention from the gay community. I was set loose in a society that accepted and wanted me. The feeling was new, exciting, and addicting.

One night as I was swiping through profiles, I matched with a guy with whom I began a conversation. We chatted for a bit, and I invited him over. That night for dinner, I'd made a Peruvian cuisine called lomo saltado. I paired it with a cosmopolitan cocktail.

When he arrived, we continued drinking and making small talk. He was very smart, and I enjoyed that our conversation moved from the basics to deeper issues like health care and politics. One drink, two drinks, three drinks, and the room began to feel hot, my words began to slur a bit, and my thoughts became less and less cohesive.

Four drinks, then five. And the poison hit. Sitting on the couch, I thought I was going to be sick just before the room began to spin out of control. I drunkenly crawled to the toilet and heaved. I continued to violently vomit, and my head began to pound with a headache so fierce I could barely keep my head in the toilet. I was miserable. I dropped to the floor going in and out of consciousness.

The guy who I'd invited over came in the bathroom with me, but I told him repeatedly to leave. He persisted in staying. I fought against him, telling him to go home. And as I was lying there, unable to move, I felt him undo my pants button as he touched me. I felt immobilized, barely awake, but I knew what was happening. I kept telling him to stop. He moved his hands over my body and put his lips up to mine. I begged him to go, though I could barely keep my eyes open. After a bit, he finally left without violation beyond touch. I remained on the bathroom floor through the night.

The next morning, I woke up next to the toilet and mustered up enough strength to slowly crawl to the couch. The soft cushions underneath me felt good after lying on the hard floor all night. I slept there for a few hours before finally moving to the air mattress in my room. I spent the rest of the day regretting my decisions the night prior. I felt violated, and I made it a point to never see that person again.

Shortly after my unfortunate encounter, I met a gay man on Tinder who also seemed firm in his Christian beliefs by explaining that he was looking for a churchgoer in his bio. I was intrigued by this combination, so I wanted to meet this guy. I was eager to talk with him about his worldview and philosophies and how he concluded that he could be both gay and a Christian. He agreed to meet with me. We met for coffee at Starbucks, and I immediately put my Baptist hat on and interrogated him.

"If the Bible is explicit on homosexuality, how can you live as a practicing homosexual and also say you're a Christian?" I asked with an accusatory tone.

"Well, does the Bible really condemn homosexuality? I think in order to claim such a bold statement you have to go back to the original text and verbiage used to understand the meaning of what was written," he replied.

I'd heard all of this before. I told him that studying the Bible the way he suggested drew a clear picture that the Bible preached against such a lifestyle.

"Let me explain," he said in a calm tone. "The word *homosexual* wasn't translated into the Bible until the mid-1900s when the Revised Standard Version mistranslated the word *arsenokoitai* to mean 'homosexual.' This loose translation confirmed the idea that homosexuality was indeed a contemptable sin to many conservative Christians."

He continued. "Two words, *arsenokoitai* and *malakoi*, are used in reference to same-sex attraction. The first, *arsenokoitai*, is a rare and confusing word among Bible scholars and translators. Paul may have coined the word from two separate words, *arsen*, meaning 'male,' and *koites*, meaning 'bed.' It is considered that the use of these words comes directly from the way they were used in Leviticus 20:13, the passage that condemned sexual acts with children as well as having sex in exchange for money, and also the passage that many evangelicals use to condemn homosexuality. Overall, the words described unlawful acts of sexual misconduct, which is not equivalent to a committed, loving, and monogamous relationship between two men.

"The other term, *malakos*, translated as 'soft,' is a term to refer to those who are weak or effeminate. In the culture of that time, this word referenced women who were seen as weak, lustful, whorish, impure, and reduced to a submissive role in sex. It was also used to characterize men who lived lives of sexual exploitation.

"These words don't define a person's sexual orientation; they describe a domineering, unequivocal role played by a person during sex."

"So, what about Sodom and Gomorrah?" I asked. "Isn't what happened pretty clear on how God feels about homosexuality?"

"You're right, it does send a clear message on how God feels about abusive, nonconsensual, lustful sexual practices. It does not, however, condemn homosexuality. In this story, we see that the men of Sodom wanted to rape Lot's guests. In other words, the major sin discussed is what we would call a gang rape, in modern terms. The Bible strongly condemns sexual immorality such as sexual abuse. But it doesn't criticize monogamous, committed, and consensual relationships, even between the same gender."

I posed a follow-up question. "Okay, so what does the Bible say about marriage? Is it not supposed to be between a man and a woman?"

"Marriage in the Bible is based on a covenant, not on gender. Marriage is not about the individuals themselves; it is about their promise to one another, vowing to engage in a monogamous, trusting relationship," he stated with ease and a kind smile.

I listened to the words that he said, but I wasn't ready to hear them with an open heart and mind. I was still stuck on twenty years of biblical teaching that had been engrained in me. Unraveling my whole philosophical system was almost an impossible task. I knew I wanted answers, but I unrealistically wanted an explanation that somehow satisfied my confusion while staying true to my roots.

I thanked him for his time and tucked our conversation in the back of my mind. What he'd said made sense, but I was almost afraid to believe him. If I believed in the Bible like he did, would I be condemning myself to hell? Remember: the Bible was black and white. You're either obedient or disobedient. Interpretations are loose, and eternal damnation was a lot to wager on an interpretation. It was easier for me not to think about it, so I let it go and focused my time on flying around and meeting people in exciting cities. In hindsight, I realized that no matter how hard we try to silence the spiritual noise in our lives, it will eventually break through.

Twenty Three

I was loving my time as a flight attendant. I traveled the world and saw places I would have never been able to see had it not been for my job. I was getting paid to travel to wonderful places like Manchester, London, Barcelona, Paris, Los Angeles, Miami, and so on, and it was a dream. Not only was the flying great, but also, I met amazing people. Working was like traveling with friends all the time. This mobile lifestyle also provided many opportunities to meet guys without the obligation to see them again.

Over the next several months, I wasted no time hooking up with random guys I met in random cities. When I arrived at the hotel, I immediately opened up Grindr and scrolled through the profiles. Sometimes there would be other crew members staying at the hotel. We would get together because of close proximity and spend the night in the sheets. Some guys I would never speak to again, but there were others with whom I'd exchange numbers and become friends.

Overall, hooking up didn't leave me happy or satisfied. I kept looking for something more. And I would often have thoughts during our sexual encounters about my choice to forsake my religion. *What if I'm wrong, and the Bible is right?* I thought as I kissed the neck of my date that night. *If I'm wrong, what will happen to this person? Will they be OK?*

Despite these questions that hounded me on a daily basis, I continued down the path I'd started because I enjoyed being in an environment of acceptance. At work, I was surrounded by gay men. I wasn't hit on by many passengers, but several coworkers caught my attention. It was always a fun surprise to walk onto the aircraft and see that a cute gay boy was working. I enjoyed my coworkers because they allowed me to be me, and that was to be a gay man without reservation.

I smiled big and twirled around as I pranced up and down the aisles making sure everyone had what they needed. Friends and coworkers encouraged me not be ashamed to live gayly and proudly. My friend and coworker Lori Bennett told me, "Be who you are, and do so unapologetically."

This was the first time in my life that I wasn't just being in the world, but I broke the mold, and I was of the world. And during this time, I had a revelation that not all non-Christian people were bad.

There was a homeless man whose name was Felix who lived near the Logan Square Blue Line station. He was no stranger to this area, and the residents were used to seeing him. He was often seen wearing pants, a long-sleeved shirt, and a beanie that covered his thick, black hair that fell past his ears. On cold days, he'd wear a large coat that he dug out of the overstuffed shopping cart he pushed around. The cart contained the tangible items he had to his name. Felix was a very nice gentleman. He'd wave and nod when people walked by if he wasn't already occupied with internal stimuli, and he was always seen with an Intelligentsia coffee cup filled with coffee. This coffee chain had a store around the corner from where the train station was, and Felix frequented this shop. When it was cold, he'd spend a few hours sitting indoors, sipping on his coffee that he'd purchased with the few cents that he had gathered from bystanders that day. The baristas were always so kind to him; other people in the community would give him clothing, shoes, or even a homecooked meal in a Tupperware container.

I saw Felix almost every day as I walked to and from the train, or I'd see him at the coffee shop or perhaps just walking down the road. One day I thought of him and what his fate was in the eyes of God. And I thought, *Who did that to him? Who gave him that life?* The mental health issues that accompanied his homelessness were certainly not a choice of his, because who would want to live like that? But without too much speculation, I begged the question "Why?"

If God is in control, and He is a loving God, why would He allow people to live like this? I talked with one of my friends about the massive homeless population in Chicago. And he told me that some of those people chose to be homeless because they didn't want to abide by the rules and regulations of the homeless shelters offering a warm and clean place to spend the night. And that was their prerogative, but the mental health issues that plagued others in that group were not something anyone wished for. These people never even had a chance, and it was like God threw them away.

A few days later, I was riding on the train back home from O'Hare, and I noticed that a nun had boarded the train. She was sitting across from me quietly reading a book. I looked at her and posed the same question I had for Felix. Being a nun, she was clearly a Catholic.

Fundamental Baptists and Catholics don't believe in the same thing. So, who's right? According to Baptists, that poor woman is headed straight for destruction. However, in her mind, she's on the straight and narrow to heaven based off of her beliefs and the good deeds that she's done on this earth—she even dedicated her entire life to be a nun for God. But since she believes in salvation through works instead of faith, then she will not inherit the kingdom of God. Would God really turn her away on judgment day? How is that kind? How is that love?

Then I turned the focus onto the people I knew and the friends that I was making. Were these seemingly wonderful people going to hell just for existing?

I had a conversation with my flight attendant friend Joy as we sat in the back galley after the drink service was completed on a flight one day. I asked her what she thought of God and religion. She told me that she had no issues with Christians or religion but that it just wasn't for her. She told me that she believed in the existence of God, but she didn't care for organized religion or going to church because evangelicals seem hypocritical and judgmental.

My other friend Josh, who is gay and the son of a pastor, left the church and his family because of mistreatment and for not being accepted. What message does that treatment send?

"If the Bible is true, then why can't evangelicals ever agree on anything?" I asked myself. The lack of continuity and disagreements surrounding the Bible and Christianity don't instill confidence in the system.

People were living their lives in the best way they knew how. They weren't hurting anyone, but were genuinely loving and kind people. And even much more so than some of the people I'd met in the church. I couldn't stomach the fact that the God I was taught about and knew would damn these people to hell just because they couldn't grasp an ambiguous truth.

Around this time, I reached out to a professor I had during college. And what he had to say challenged my thinking, a little more than I wanted.

Twenty Four

M r. Jones taught my college English 101 and literature class. He was well-respected on campus for his genuine love and kindness towards those he met. He always started his classes by singing a hymn that he chose and then a short prayer. He was energetic and laughed a lot. His intelligence amazed me, and I wanted to learn as much as I could from him. He was a very righteous man, but he did not make a habit of judging people for their sin. He treated everyone with love and respect. During this time, I reached out to him. I wanted to pick his brain about the things I was going through. And I knew that he would speak to me in a meaningful and graceful way. Our conversation, which I'll share here, was an impactful tool in my journey.

I wrote to Mr. Jones:

Allowing myself to be real and unveiling thoughts and feelings about my struggle with same-sex attraction has brought into question my whole worldview. I will get right to the point and say that coming to terms with who I am, dealing with deep personal issues, and witnessing how the world lives, has made me question the character of God. If God is sovereign, omnipotent, omniscient, and so on, then He is in control of everything, and nothing happens without His approval first. With that said, all the good, the bad, and the ugly has God's stamp of approval on it. And the reality of what He allows produces some very harsh results. I don't believe that people are innately bad; I believe that people are doing the best they can with what they have. Everyone is trying his or her hardest to make it from one day to the next because we're so lost and hurt, and we're just trying to find solace somewhere. God is an anomaly to most people. And people associate Christianity with a set of rules and cult-like behavior. Furthermore, Christians get a bad reputation of judgment, hate, backbiting, and finger-pointing. Even if that's not completely accurate, the few bad apples ruin it for the rest.

I have dealt with so much hurt and pain my entire life. I have never felt like I fit in anywhere. I always felt broken because I could never eradicate myself from the horrible awful struggle I dealt with deep inside. In our circles, being gay was the worst thing anyone could do, and that's who I was! And it terrified me. All this fostered stress, anxiety, depression, bitterness, constantly feeling like a failure because I always fell into my desires. And that made me feel like I was letting myself down as well as others around me.

The problem with ABC circles is that I felt like their version of Christianity focused more on outward appearance rather than the heart. If you weren't living the model Christian life, then there was an issue with your salvation. This mindset, accompanied with all my other doubts, weighed on my mind and heart, compelling me to do whatever it took to look like the best Christian. The more Christian things I did, the more Christian I was supposed to feel. In return, the more Christian I looked, the more approval I gained from others.

But still, nothing abated my inner turmoil. I also thought that the more Christian I tried to be, the less I would struggle. That's a lot of the reason I became a *missionary* to Peru. Actually serving the Lord on the mission field would definitely gain me hefty points. Not to mention all the applause I would get from others. All that would definitely assuage my empty, disgusted, anxious heart.

Twenty years of constant battle. Hating myself. Distancing myself. Growing in bitterness and anguish. Twenty years trying to find peace, understanding, comfort, and rest. I looked in all the places I was told to look—but I found nothing except more struggle, depression, and anxiety because what I wanted wasn't where it was supposed to be.

So I made the decision to leave Peru and start looking elsewhere. That journey unveiled so many more thoughts and brought up so many more questions, which circles me back around to my first paragraph—Why doesn't God make sense?

Mr. Jones:

Hey, my friend! This is a lot to think about. Excellent stuff so far, Jordan. I just wish you had opened up to me about all this earlier, but I'm sure you would have been fearing a judgmental attitude. You wouldn't have found one, and you won't now. All of us humans struggle with this obviously broken life, both externally and internally. Constantly. Yeah, me too. Will tell you more about my personal struggles later—which, by the way, change with age.

What I want you to know is that I totally get your viewpoint. You are describing exactly what the world looks like from a completely human perspective (bear in mind that I'm a human too and can see this as plain as day). If all we can see and feel with the world in its present condition is all we get, then life sucks, and we might as well focus on self and get as much pleasure as we can because this is a nightmare planet. Death, disease, hatred, violence, loss, fear, betrayal—yikes! Get me outta this! What kind of God is running this show anyhow?

And your view of and experience with Christianity (along with the experiences and views of most everyone both living and dead) have not been happy. Just looks like a bunch of external posturing. With all this, your observations are dead on. What I can do is tell you how I will approach it and give you one important assurance.

First, you know I will approach it all from a biblical standpoint, for as distasteful as it seems to the world, my experience with my brokenness and the messed-up world I live in have shown me that the Bible tells the truth on me, the world, God, and the way life works.

Second, I will not approach Christianity as a set of externals, but rather a relationship. No matter what we look like on the outside, Jesus made it plain in Mark 7 that external matters very little. I invite you to read that chapter over. I'm sad that the majority of those who say they are Christians and the majority of parachurch organizations, like Bible colleges and mission agencies, focus on the externals. They are wrong.

Finally, an assurance: I don't see sexual preference as the "worst thing anyone can do," as you put it. There is only one unforgivable sin: rejecting the Person and work of the Lord Jesus Christ on the behalf of every individual who has ever and will ever live. There are plenty of other problems each of us struggles with as well.

Jordan, this world is disappointing because it is not Home. This is not what we were meant for. No wonder we're uncomfortable and dissatisfied here!

May I ask you a question to get my bearings a little? Do you believe any of the Bible now? Do you believe there is a God or eternal life? If that sounds smart alecky, I don't mean it to be. Based on your honest statements, it would just help me to know that.

Jordan:

It has never been nor ever will be my intention to offend you in any way. I know that your answers are genuine and that I don't have to fear judgment from you. This is what sets you apart from so many other people I have known. And you're right, this is a nightmare planet; it's a nightmare system that results in more tragedy than good.

I don't know what I believe about the Bible anymore. However, I do know that what I see in my own life, and what's going on in the world is not consistent with who God says He is. So, if God is flawed (and I believe He is), then I can't take the Bible to be infallible.

Now, I also can't believe there isn't some intelligent design happening. Even as I study the human body, I have to wonder that we're more than blobs of chemicals walking around.

I feel like God has placed us in this torturous game of life without our permission, turned us loose, and said, "Good luck!" Only a few will get out alive. May the odds be ever in your favor.

I know that may sounds cheesy, and I did borrow that from the Hunger Games, but that's how I feel life is.

Mr. Jones:

I have been casting about in my mind as to how to begin to share with you after your honest sharing with me. Not sure I will do this right, but here goes. It seems to me that what you're saying comes down to dissatisfaction with God, the religion of Christianity (I put religion in there on purpose), as well as a resultant dismissal of the Bible. I do understand. All I can tell you is what a relationship—not a religion—with God and His Son has done for me.

I'm probably not a typical Christian in a lot of ways, but I think the main way is that I don't think of myself as mainly a guy who keeps the rules God has laid down, but a privileged adopted son of my heavenly Father. He has given me peace and purpose in my life, and a lot of joy. Joy is not always happiness, but an abiding calm and the ability to trust a Person Who is wiser, stronger, and more loving than I will ever be.

Jordan, I have never suffered in this life, so I know my viewpoint may seem skewed to many. I have never been hungry to the point of starvation or illness. I have never been tortured or beaten up because of my faith. I'm not a quadriplegic or a paraplegic. I've always had a nice place to live and nice clothes to wear. I have always had way more than enough money to live well, except perhaps when Donna and I were first married. I've never had cancer (save for a small spot on my nose that was easily removed). I was born with good health that continues to this day and a fairly good mind that has allowed me to understand a lot and even share it with others. My ability to think and share has, most of the time, spared me the dilemma of always being at the mercy of my emotions, which are not pretty.

Since I have brought that up, let me confess that I have anger management problems, am fearful, very selfish, proud, and lazy. I'm lustful in the sexual sense. I have tried giving in to all those emotions in the past; not a one of them gives me satisfaction, but all have worked to take away my peace and joy. So I'm thankful for the supernatural help Father has given me to, most of the time, keep all that me stuff under control. Otherwise, I would currently be very ill, dead, or in jail.

I have suffered one great tragedy, the homegoing of my life companion after forty-six years of marriage. So, in spite of my privileged life, I do understand a little about loss, grief, and terrible emotional pain.

Now I also understand how Father has helped me through this pain. Oh, I was yelling at Him and beating on His chest even as He held me close to comfort me. But eventually I came to see that He was just as sad as I, even sadder, at not only my loss, but at the terrible mess the whole world is in. It's not like He never warned us that things would be hard. One of the very last things that Jesus told us before He was arrested and tortured to death was that "in the world, you will have tribulation." He also told us to have a close relationship with Him, we would have to deny ourselves and take up our cross.

In first-century terms, He said, "To have a close relationship with Me, you will have to die to self and suffer torture." Yeah, I know: Who wants to sign up for that? But He also has said, "Be happy—I have overcome the world!" Really? Then why did my Donna die of cancer in less than five months? I still don't know the answer to that one, really, though I have a good guess as to one reason. More about that later, perhaps.

But the fact is that through this terrible loss, He showed Himself the closest, most caring Friend I could ever imagine. He kept me sane, He protected me from bitterness, and He allowed me to keep my joy (remember, not always happiness). He reminded me that I'm not the only one to lose a life companion, but that I still had a Friend "who sticks closer than a brother." And He has assured me, in spite of my complaints, mistrust, and fearfulness, that He will still use me if I let Him.

In short, He has amazed me with His love and care.

See, that's not religion. That is a relationship. Religion is hollow and impersonal and is simply keeping the rules and hoping one is doing the rule-keeping well enough to satisfy a stern, judgmental God. It is also thinking that if one does keep those rules well enough, God will give us whatever we see as blessing.

But a relationship with Him, well, that's a whole different story. It never has involved getting what I thought I needed to have. You know my story: I wanted to be a test pilot and an astronaut. God took my eyesight and denied me that desire, and I was angry with Him for a long time. But I have come to realize that if I'd gotten what I wanted, I wouldn't be who I am today. I would quite possibly be dead or disabled, and probably would have spent time in the Hanoi Hilton during the Vietnam War. At the very least, I know I would have become career Air Force and thus wouldn't have been a prof at ABC, meaning I would never have even known you, my friend, and would have never know the satisfaction of knowing real purpose and joy in my life.

As it turns out, even if I don't understand, Father is a lot smarter than me. He has told me that to trust my own understanding is dangerous and even foolish, and that if I commit (finally!) my way to Him, He will direct my paths. And He has. I got to know you and your family, haven't I? And have I ever flown? Did He deny that to me completely? No. I have been in the air in the cockpits of some of the most amazing and important aircraft to ever fly. I have flown Delta's flight simulators and piloted a CRJ. I have soloed twice. I have been in the cockpit of a P-51D, for crying out loud. No, Father takes care of His adopted kids when they let Him lead.

As for the mess the world is in, He cries over that too, because it does not please Him. But He told us the reason: He gave us free choice, and look what we did with it. I know I would have done no better in the Garden of Eden than Adam and Eve, and now, because of the rebellion that they exercised with their free choice, I have that spirit of rebellion in me. So every day, it is a struggle with myself to stay lovingly obedient to Father. It's not easy, but the peace and joy are well worth the struggle.

The close relationship with Him through His Son is worth it. You may remember that I often said, "Getting to know the Lord Jesus Christ does not happen on the way to a ministry; ministry is what happens on the way to getting to know the Lord Jesus Christ." He is the Center, the most important Person in the universe. Not me. And by surrendering to that, He freely gives me Himself, which is joy and peace. Not religion. Him.

Jordan:

Thank you for sharing those thoughts with me. I appreciate your candor. People don't believe because they don't understand truth.

We cannot forget that sin has blinded everyone, and no one can believe/know the truth unless God wills them to come to Him. Sadly, that's not the ending of many people's stories.

I want to know why people don't believe. Believers would say the world doesn't believe because of its sin and rebellion. I say that people don't willingly choose their destiny. I mean, who would choose hell over heaven? The people who I have come to know and love are not bad people. They are the models of love, goodness, and care. And you also demonstrate all those things and more, my friend.

God has made it so difficult for average people to know Him. I won't even go into the array of religions and belief systems people dedicate their lives to because that's what they call truth. People put their complete faith in something that has no good return. Who put those thoughts in their minds? No one understands what's going on. So how are we punished for something we don't get? Wasn't it Jesus who said, "Father, forgive them; they know *no* what they *do*." They didn't get it then, and we still don't get it now. We are intelligent creatures. Why is our fate based in something so obscure? We are asked to believe something that goes against our nature/intelligence. The story of Jesus just doesn't make logical sense when compared to the present world. I don't doubt His existence, but His purpose in relation to our reality doesn't connect the dots.

To me, it's seems that if God loved us so much, then the All-Powerful could have designed a better plan that produced a better outcome. I will take the focus off of my peers and put it on myself for a minute.

I didn't ask to be born the way I am with the struggles I have. I didn't ask to be plagued with worrisome amounts of anxiety and depression. I didn't ask for the pain and confusion caused by growing up as a gay man in a legalistic world. I didn't ask for any of it. As a matter of fact, no one has asked to be here. No one has requested their destiny. We are here as a result of the Sovereign One's messy game. We're all just living, trying to make it from one day to the next. And for most of us, this is as good as it's going to get. Whose fault is that?

I'm deeply sorry for your loss, something I cannot even begin to empathize with. But you're one of the chosen. You've been granted that joy and peace that overwhelms you when the pain of this life attacks. You have purpose. I envy you. So why you and not me? Why me and not others? I hate this agony.

Mr. Jones:

> Jordan, I believe that God does have a better ending than what we see here. It's the restoration of all things as He meant them to be. As I wrote in an earlier message, this is not Home. Also, I believe that God deals with individuals. If you do know His message, then you have the free will to make a choice concerning that knowledge. In fact, if you know the message, you cannot help but make a choice about it. I don't understand why I have peace and joy because I certainly don't deserve it based on my big, obvious faults, but I do know this: when I face Him at the bema on judgment day, He will not ask me about you. And He will not ask you about me. He will only deal with the decisions we make based on what we know. I hate your agony too, my friend, and I believe Father does as well.

> Just a thought or two that occurred to me this morning. You feel that God is not fair in even creating us, to have put us here without our permission. To me, the fact that He as the Creator God has indeed put me here just underscores the fact that this is His game, His universe. That means I have to play my life by the directions He has given. I'm very imperfect in seeking to do that, but I have sought to do so.

> As I described earlier, for this pitiful effort, He has given me joy and peace. And I have seen the unhappiness in the lives of those who refuse to try. He doesn't expect perfection from us; He wants our love and obedience, the opposite of rebellion. Again, it's a relationship with Him, not perfectly keeping the rules.

> To me, if He is indeed God and I'm simply created by Him, then my job is not to give Him advice (though He deigns to listen to me when I do, even when the pot talks back to the Potter); my job is to obey and "walk humbly with my God," as Solomon wrote. You are right: we're here in this mess, and we can do nothing about it. But fighting God is a waste of time and energy. He will always win. So why not play by His rules? It is indeed His universe.

Also, do you really want God to be fair? If He were, I would have been in hell a long time ago. If He were, the human race wouldn't exist. No, I don't want fair from God—I want mercy and grace. And that's what I have personally experienced. If I thought that this place is the end of His plan, I would have given up totally after Donna's death. But the biggest part of His plan is that life here is temporary and the permanent life I will live in eternity in "a new heaven and a new earth where righteousness dwells" is what I wait for, not to be fulfilled here. That's mercy, not fairness. I trust His love and wisdom in His plan for me. That, I think, is the key to my joy and peace. Without trusting Him, those two things would be impossible for me.

I wrestled with everything that Mr. Jones had eloquently and clearly explained in his responses because it was all information that I'd heard before. My heart was heavy. If he was right in everything that he said, and I chose to believe it, then I would have to forsake my being gay and deal with the misery of denying myself the physical relationships, love, and ultimately marriage with the gender I was attracted to. If he was right and I chose against what he said, then I would go to hell when I died. So, even if I did choose to live freely as a gay man, this overbearing idea that I was destined for hell lingered in my mind like a warning sign that wouldn't shut off. I felt like I lost no matter what. I wanted to be free, but this spiritual torment raged in my heart.

That night, I texted a few friends to see if they wanted to go out. We immediately planned and met in Boystown (the gayborhood in Chicago) to let off some steam and hopefully quiet my turbulent heart. My goal was to turn off that pesky warning sign. It was a weekday, so the clubs were not too crowded. We met at Sidetrack and entered the bar together. The music was loud, and there was a red hue across the room from the assortment of lights. We sat at the main bar in the center of the club. This was a safe place. Everywhere I looked there were people like me or people who accepted me. We started with a tequila shot and yelled, "Arriba, abajo, al centro, pa' dentro!" and down it went.

After a few more shots, we danced to the music with each other as we laughed and talked about relationships, work, and how hot the guys across the room were. By 2:00 a.m., we shut down the bar and stumbled onto the street. I got my phone out, which looked like two in my hand as I tried to focus. The lights were blurry, and I squinted to find the Uber app. I made it home and passed out in bed with my clothes and jacket on.

Chapter Twenty Five

One of the biggest struggles I felt at this time was not measuring up to the person everyone else expected me to be. When I'd left my parents' house and moved to Chicago, I was free to be openly gay; however, I quickly realized that there was still an expectation that others had over me.

For example, as I was learning about gay relationships, I discovered the roles of a top and a bottom. In most situations, the top would take on a more masculine role while the bottom reflected a more feminine role.

When people interacted with me, they automatically assumed that I was the feminine one. Sounds familiar. They put me in the box that gay society deemed appropriate for me. But that wasn't the box I wanted to be in. I didn't enjoy being a bottom during sex. But I was embarrassed to say so because I didn't want people to oppose me. During many of the hookups I'd had, the guy I was with would treat me as a bottom, saying things like, "All I want to do is top you" except in more colorful language. I felt like I would never be enough if I wasn't the person they wanted or expected me to be.

One particular night that changed my life took place in October 2017. I had a long layover in Austin. I knew a guy who was there at the same time, so I messaged him and invited him over. A few hours later, I met him at the hotel bar for a drink. He worked at a different airline, and I'd met him through mutual friends. We engaged in small talk about the weather and swapped stories about unruly passengers and extended flight delays. I was drinking margaritas that night, and before I knew it, two of them had evaporated. The bartender was generous on the pours. With tequila in my bloodstream, I loosened up and felt a rush of ecstasy and spontaneity that often comes with drinking. We ordered a third cocktail and played footsy under the bar as we made eye contact, silently communicating what we wanted to happen next. As we talked, he gently stroked my arm with his hand. After we finished our cocktails, he mentioned ending the night in my room. I gave him a scolding but playful look. We clinked our glasses together and threw back the last gulp. The check was paid, and we stumbled through the hotel as I showed him to my room.

We began to make out as soon as we got through the door. Our clothes came off one article at a time until I found myself lying on the bed with him on top of me. But I told him that I didn't want to go that far, meaning penetration. Despite my disapproval, I felt him push harder. At that point, I was too scared to say anything, so I said nothing at all. I silently begged for it to end. I remember his face. His expression was one of enjoyment as I lay there tensed bearing the pain I felt. His breath was labored and in sync with his thrusting motion. He closed his eyes and let out a resolute sigh as he smiled and tilted his head back. It was over. He hovered over me on all fours and smiled; then gave me a gentle slap on the cheek and said, "You're cute." I flinched and turned my head away. He rolled off me, put on his clothes while he told me he'd text me later and then left. I never responded to his texts

I felt a void in my soul where only the deepest and blackest feelings reside. I ached from a place I cannot describe. I could feel a physical rawness that I knew wasn't right. I went to the bathroom and turned on the shower. I took a piece of toilet paper and dabbed my backside; when I looked, I saw red stains on the tissue. My anxiety immediately elevated.

With my back against the bathroom wall, I slid down into a seated position. I brought my arms close to my chest and rested my chin in the palm of my hands as I rocked myself back and forth for a few minutes as I processed what had happened. I took a shower but couldn't seem to scrub off the dirtiness I felt. I was sickened to my core. I knew something physical was wrong. I just didn't know what.

A few months later, I noticed some physical discomfort in my rectal area, so I went to my doctor who examined me and referred me to a colorectal surgeon. The surgeon examined me and told me that I have an aggressive disease which is manifesting in physical symptoms. The diagnosis and persistent follow-up visits (including surgery) served as a catalyst for stress and anxiety. After delivering the news, he walked toward the door of the exam room and as he opened it, he turned to me and said, "Oh, do you have any questions?"

Stunned by what had just happened, I shook my head no, and he walked out the door.

The appointments, the procedures, and the other stressors in life made me so anxious that I was prescribed Xanax to help calm my anxiety. About a week later, I went to the hospital to have a procedure with local anesthetic. As I lay on the table on my side, I felt humiliated and vulnerable. I remember looking over at the nurse who was charting at a computer. She was so kind. I focused on her as the burning continued. I wanted her to hold my hand, but I was too shy to ask. Once the procedure was completed, she helped me off the table and escorted me into another room where I could get dressed. She brought me some water and asked if I had any questions. I said "no" and was discharged from the hospital.

Since then, I had to attend appointments every three months for the next year, two of which included more procedures. From then on, I didn't engage in sexual activities which required me to bottom. First, I needed time to physically heal; the scars remained and caused pain. Second, the emotional trauma of sex was too great to bear. So, I took a break for a while.

In April of 2017, my friend, Brittany, who I came to know well through work, took me out for dinner and a movie for my birthday. Brittany was a beautiful young woman with a bubbly spirit. We flew many trips together. She often asked me about growing up gay in a Baptist family, which I gladly spoke about. She asked because she wanted to learn. And she'd always conclude with, "You are so special, Jordan. And I love you."

After the birthday dinner, we headed to the movie theatre to see *Love, Simon* as it had just come out. Afterward, I was so empowered and encouraged that I immediately grabbed my phone, opened the Facebook app, and started typing up a dramatically victorious coming-out post. I'd been out to my friends in Chicago, but the situation with my family hadn't changed. I still hadn't spoken with my siblings about my decision and many people from my past also were not aware of my new lifestyle. So, when everything was just right, I hit the share button with both apprehension and excitement. Moments later, a barrage of likes and comments flooded my new post.

As you can imagine from colliding both of my worlds, I received feedback from both sides. I received comments like, "Only the Bible is truth," or "We will be praying for you." I expected these types of replies. Then I got a reply from one of my music professors that was unexpected, encouraging and insightful. I will share that interaction here.

> Professor: We are all on a beautiful journey to find God and to find ourselves in relationship to God and our fellow man. I'll be praying for you on what undoubtedly will be a rocky road for a while after coming out. But congrats on taking this step. You are made in the image of God, your Creator and Sustainer.

> Me: Along this journey, we find that God is a little bit different for each individual, and I guess that's OK. It's all a big mess, really, but we're surviving. And you're right, this has been a rocky road from the beginning of time.

> Professor: God is the same God, I believe, but God has a personal relationship with each of us. And no two of us are alike!

A few months after the social media reveal, my family and I congregated at my sister's house for a weekend getaway. I don't remember the specific reason, but it must have been important enough for me to fly down from Chicago to hang out with my family; this would be the first time we were all together since 2016. I felt nervous that there would be some heavy debates over the weekend, but I was ready to stand on my own two feet and defend the choices I'd made.

One evening, such a debate broke out. I was sitting in my sister's living room when my sister came and sat next to me. We carried on a casual conversation. She asked about my living in Chicago and if I was enjoying my job. I told her that things were going well, and that I was enjoying traveling around the world. At this point, my mom stepped into the conversation. My sister then asked me how my relationship with God was.

My brother-in-law and dad walked in. I remember one of them saying, "Oh, this sounds like a deep conversation." They both sat down and listened to my response.

I told her that I wasn't sure about what I believed about God. I told her that I struggled with being a Christian because I couldn't measure up to the standard set before me. I asked her a lot of the question I'd discussed with the college prof. I explained that I was taking time to step back and question my faith. And for the present time, I was living my life without the influence of religion or claiming the Bible as my truth. I took a deep breath and said that I wanted to be my true self. I said that I identified as gay, and I was ready to accept that.

At that point, my sister told me that she had read my Facebook post and had taken it hard. She told me that she was offended that I didn't tell her personally and asked why. I didn't have a good answer to her question.

My sister and mom told me that they loved me and that nothing would ever change, but they couldn't accept my lifestyle because it went directly against the teaching of the Bible. It was said that God and our relationship with Him is the most important thing in this life, even more important than family.

The most impactful thing my sister said during that conversation was this: "Jordan, let me ask you a question. If you're right by saying that the Bible isn't true, then I, as a believer, have nothing to lose, and you have nothing to lose when we die. But if I'm right, and the Bible is true, then I still have nothing to lose and everything to gain, but where does that leave you?"

I knew she was indirectly asking where I would spend eternity. I said, "Well, what if we're both right?"

And she said, "That scenario doesn't exist."

Throughout that conversation, I felt like I wasn't being heard. Rather, I was being admonished. The primary focus was sin, and the goal was to talk me about of my sinful behaviors without trying to understand the weight of the burden or what it was really like to be a gay man. I didn't want to have to debate or defend my position as a gay man to my family.

I just wanted to be accepted for who God made me to be. But because of their faithfulness to the Lord and their interpretation of the Bible, acceptance of me wasn't an option. They could, however, love me, pray for me, and continue to send me Bible verses, sermon series, and podcasts about turning from a gay lifestyle.

Overall, I took their words to heart as I continued to battle my place in this world. I wanted it to be easy, but it wasn't. It was all so confusing, and I wanted it to make sense. I couldn't figure out why it didn't. Maybe I didn't really want a God who I could understand.

Over time, I started to get bored with flying. I felt like I wanted more out of my job. I wanted to feel accomplished at the end of the day, but doing a beverage service and telling people to buckle their seatbelts wasn't giving me the satisfaction I was looking for. Of course, it was nice that the job was easy and traveling was fun, but I yearned for something more. And it wasn't long before I found just the thing I needed.

Chapter Twenty Six

As I completed my second year of flying, I realized that customer service didn't make me happy. While seeing the world was extraordinary, it didn't fulfill my soul. I was burned out from the job. I was astounded by how rude and belligerent passengers could be toward one another and the flight crew. I remember one flight I worked on the 787 Dreamliner from Chicago to Los Angeles. I worked first class, and there was a man sitting in the last row of my aisle in first class. When we reached cruising altitude, my colleague and I went into the aisles to present the two options we had for dinner that night, a grilled chicken with a side of vegetables, or four-cheese ravioli. We started at the front and worked our way back. As I reached the last row, I apologized to the passengers that all we had left was the ravioli. One passenger became upset that the chicken option was no longer available. I apologized again, but the passenger spoke over me reiterating how poorly the airline was functioning and wasted no time expressing his anger and frustration.

With hopes to appease this disgruntled passenger, I went to the back and gathered an assortment of sandwiches, cookies, hummus plates, and other items to present to the passenger in first class.

When I returned to the passenger, he said, "What is this?"

I said, "Well, I'm sorry that we couldn't give you what you wanted, so I got a few things from the back that I thought you might enjoy instead."

The passenger have me a blank look and said, "No, thank you."

His rejection upset me, especially after I'd gone above and beyond to try and help him. Then I realized that some people will always choose negativity, no matter what you do for them.

The interactions were not enjoyable for me because I took them home and ruminated on them. I let the negative situations fester until they began to affect my thoughts and attitude. At that point, I knew I needed to make a change.

I realized that I didn't want to make a career out of flying, and nursing came racing back to my mind. I began researching schools in the area with programs that would fit my schedule. The programs I was looking into required several prerequisites before starting the program such as biology, two classes of anatomy and physiology, chemistry, and microbiology. So I took these classes online while I worked full-time. It worked out because I could do my homework while I sat on the on the aircraft and during my layovers. Over the next year, I completed all the courses required to apply to the programs I was interested in.

During the spring of 2018, I applied to three schools in the Chicago area. Of the three schools, I ending up choosing to study at DePaul University. I was scheduled to start fall 2018, and I couldn't wait.

I wasn't able to work full-time and attend in-person classes, especially since my flying schedule was inconsistent. After a lot of work and advocacy on behalf of my manager, I was granted an education leave while I was in school. And during my breaks, I would work.

My two years of school went by quickly. I met incredible people and had a wonderful experience. Dr. Kim Amer was one of my professors whom I connected with the most. Through our interactions together, Dr. Amer made me feel wanted and accepted. She invested in me because she saw potential and called me worthy. I remember walking by her office one day and noticing an LGBTQ+ sticker on her door, which gave me great confidence knowing that she was an ally.

We didn't have a formal graduation because of the COVID-19 pandemic. We, like so many other students, graduated online. For me, it was still very special, and I couldn't believe my accomplishments. I often told people that I almost didn't even apply to nursing school because I didn't believe that I was smart enough or good enough to pass my classes and graduate. Not only did I graduate, but also I did with a nearly perfect GPA. And that isn't because I'm smart, but because I worked hard and studied until I knew the material. And then kept studying.

Chapter Twenty Seven

Once I graduated, I wasted no time taking my boards. The night before the exam, I tossed and turned from anxiety.

What if I fail? I thought. It all boils down to one test. I'm literally putting all my eggs into one basket. My test was scheduled for 10:00 a.m. My alarm clock went off at 8:00 a.m., but I was already wide awake. I took a shower, fixed myself a light breakfast, and looked over a few more practice questions as I picked at the bagel I'd toasted. But I didn't have much of an appetite. I brushed my teeth and was out the door by 9:00 a.m.

I walked three minutes to the Blue Line train station at Logan Square for the train downtown. The testing center was on the corner of Adams and Wells streets. I had no problem finding the center as I knew downtown very well.

I walked into the training center and everything was very stoic and procedural. The secretary requested all the necessary documents in a monotone, routine way. This wasn't a master class in customer service. She made copies of my ID and told me to sit down and wait for my name to be called. There were four other people in the waiting are with me. I overheard one person saying they were taking the MCAT, and another person said they were taking the NCLEX. I quietly looked around feeling my stomach turning.

Then I heard my name called. I was ushered into a room where my fingerprints were taken, then I was instructed to put all of my belongings in a marked locker. I was given some headphones and escorted to the computer where I'd be tested on my knowledge of nursing. Here I was sitting for the NCLEX. I took a deep breath and clicked Begin.

A couple days later, I was informed by the learning center that I'd passed the NCLEX. To say I was relieved would be an understatement. I immediately called my parents and, with tears in my eyes, told them the good news. They celebrated with me over the phone and told me how proud they were. They were proud of my professional accomplishments, but their acceptance of my being gay was still a sore subject. In fact, we just didn't talk about it. There were many times when I would have loved to share that part of my life with my parents like J did with his, but I knew that we weren't on those terms. My parents and I agreed to disagree and left it there.

Because of the pandemic, most airline employees had been furloughed, including myself. Luckily for me, I had nursing to fall back on, but I knew many friends who did not have a stable job to lean on during this unprecedented and scary time.

After passing the NCLEX, I immediately started looking for jobs, which weren't hard to find. I wanted to start working as soon as possible. My first nursing job was at Northwestern Memorial Hospital in downtown Chicago. This was my dream job.

When I was a new Chicago resident, I spent many days walking through downtown, exploring my new home. On one of my explorations, I stumbled upon the Northwestern University campus. I admired all of the flowers and the perfectly manicured landscape that enhanced the buildings and presence of the campus. I then found the immaculate hospital. I looked up at the tall structure and thought, *I want to work here someday.*

Four years later, I was sitting in a Zoom meeting interviewing for a position in the liver/kidney transplant unit. A few days later, I received a call from the HR department with a job offer. I accepted and began my preceptorship a few weeks after.

All nurses are set up with a preceptor and orientation that lasts anywhere from eight to twelve weeks. At Northwestern, the orientation was twelve weeks. During this time, we learned the fundamentals of nursing while under the careful watch of a preceptor, a teacher or trainer.

My preceptor, Cassie, was incredible. We became great friends the first day we met; I will be forever grateful for everything she taught me and the loving, compassionate care she extended to each and every one of her patients. She is the epitome of a great nurse—full of knowledge, education, patience, and compassion.

Cassie did a wonderful job easing me into the role and teaching me what I needed to know to be successful as a transplant nurse. Our days were filled with laughter and joy as we worked together toward the common goal of healthy outcomes. She was tough on me, but her constructive criticism came in a loving way that fostered growth and learning. She created an environment conducive for asking questions, making mistakes, and improving my skills on a daily basis.

I remember one day Cassie and I were working, and we had a patient who had come in to the hospital for a kidney transplant. This patient had just returned from surgery a few hours prior and was in significant pain. The patient had an order for medication. So I retrieved the vial from the medication dispenser, brought it to the patient's room, scanned it into the computer, drew it up in a syringe, and pushed it through the IV. The patient thanked me. I nodded with a smile and walked out feeling so good that I was learning how to be a good nurse, and I was helping people at the same time.

I found Cassie and told that I'd given the patient medication feeling very good about showing initiative. She then looked at me and said, "That's great. Where's the rest of it?"

There was a pause. And I got that nasty feeling in my stomach like I'd done something terribly wrong.

"Um." I muttered.

"You gave it all, didn't you?" she replied, already knowing the answer.

We both went to check on the patient, who was fine, and monitored them until the effects of the drug wore off. We then took the necessary steps of admitting my error to the charge nurse.

Cassie demonstrated her patience by kindly helping me through the process of learning rather than scolding me for a job horribly done. Since then, I have learned to be very detailed and precise in my nursing practice. I have not made a medication error since.

While my orientation was done on days, I was hired to work nights. So, once my training was complete, I started the night shift grind. The night shift crew and I meshed well. Not only did we enjoy working together, but we frequently gathered outside of work as a way to relieve stress and build our relationships. I've found that those who hang out together outside of work have better teamwork.

One of my favorite pastimes was going out to brunch after a night shift. There was a place we frequently went to near the hospital called Kanela. We'd order breakfast and a carafe of mimosas while we laughed and talked about life and work. We bonded over every patient cleanup, crazy work assignments, and the interesting patients we encountered. We were a family.

One evening we all got together to have dinner and drinks at a familiar place in Chicago called Offshore. This was a beautiful restaurant at the end of Navy Pier. And there is a view of the skyline that makes for excellent photo backgrounds. We were shown to our table which had several large chairs with comfy cushions surrounding a medium-sized, rectangular coffee table. We ordered a few appetizers and margaritas, then posed together for a photoshoot, yielding more than enough photos to spice up our Tinder profiles.

We laughed our way through the evening joking about work and how grateful we were for one another. I remember at one point I squeezed into a big chair with my friends Rachel and Elyse as we gave a "cheers" and took a shot of tequila. We hugged each other tightly because that's the type of friends we were. We stayed at Offshore until they closed and were all but kicked out.

One of our coworkers had a two-bedroom condo in downtown Chicago. The place was gorgeous with updated appliances, floor-to-ceiling windows that overlooked the city and a balcony where you could sit outside and take in the magnificent views of the sun rising over Lake Michigan, weather permitting. She invited us all over to spend the night, which was something we did more than once. We drunkenly found ourselves an Uber and made it to her place. Somehow, White Claws found themselves into our hands, and we played music through the night until we noticed that the sun was coming up through the big windows in the living room. We conquered the night and planned for brunch. We walked over to Yolk café, looking like we had just drunk all night, which is accurate. By the time we sat down and ordered coffee, the hangover feeling hit us all. Without even touching our food, we requested the bill and made our way home.

There was one night at work that was particularly busy. We had a lot of post-transplant patients who needed care, and then we were slammed with several admissions overnight. It was one of those nights where I was able to go to the bathroom maybe twice in a twelve-hour shift. In the middle of the shift, I remember all of us coming together in a circle putting our hands in the middle and saying in a rhythmic motion, "We will eat tonight," signifying that amid the chaos, we would find time to eat dinner. We worked well together. I couldn't have asked for a better crew to begin my nursing career with.

I didn't mind working the night shift. I actually preferred it because it was a slower pace. However, the wake-sleep cycle was difficult on my body and mind. Over time, I began to feel the emotional pangs of working that schedule. I was missing the sun. When I woke up, it was only a matter of hours before everyone else was getting ready for bed. When I wasn't working, I found myself alone in my apartment trying to keep myself awake during the greater part of the night. Even though my co-workers and I were close, our schedules didn't always line up. And while we enjoyed hanging out and did so whenever we could, it didn't always happen. I became very lonely.

My good friend Mattie from nursing school and I worked the same night schedules but at different hospitals. We helped each other stay awake by texting. And we talked about everything from our jobs to life to the shows we were watching. One particular show we were watching at the time was *Port Protection*. The show was about people who live to survive in a rural area of Alaska called Port Protection. The people who live in this portion of Alaska hunt for food, build their own houses, and live simple lives outside of society. Mattie and I joked that we wouldn't even survive two days in the bush, but we did enjoy watching others do it.

Another way I tried to occupy my time during the night was to bake. I enjoyed baking and thought I would dabble in some cake decorating again. I made cupcakes with rainbow-colored icing for Pride month. I bought some cookbooks on how to make the best cakes and ones with other secret baking tips. I made a Boston cream cake that resembled a Boston cream pie. I also tried a recipe for a three-layered snickerdoodle cake, which turned out to be one of my favorites.

Several months prior, I'd connected with a guy, Lukas. He worked for Delta as a flight attendant at the time, and we met through mutual friends. We followed each other on Instagram and had sent messages back and forth. Lukas was a master baker. He learned from his mom growing up and made it quite a hobby as an adult. One evening I was attempting to make cinnamon rolls that weren't turning out the way I'd hoped. So I messaged Lukas for some help. We FaceTimed each other, and he walked me through the whole process. After my dough had risen, it was time to knead it. Well, my mind went right back to the *I Love Lucy* episode I'd watched over and over again with Alyssa when Lucy learns how to make bread. When she kneads the dough, she gracefully pats the dough with her hand and then moves in from side to side on the counter.

While on FaceTime with Lukas, I dumped the dough out of the bowl and onto a floured surface on the counter. I started to press down on it with my hands and rolled it around the counter.

I remember Lukas instructing, "That's not kneading it!" with a playful tone as he laughed at my attempt. Before long, I put the cinnamon rolls in the oven and eagerly watched through the glass window on the oven door as they baked to perfection. The smell of cinnamon and bread permeated the whole house. It was a proud moment for me.

A few months later, I reached out to Lukas and asked if he wanted to come over and bake. He agreed and met me at my house with a bag full of baking supplies. I couldn't wait to get started. He was going to teach me how to make a choux pastry. As we started, we opened a bottle of rosé and turned on some French music from Spotify. Lukas was both attractive and kind, which made him even more attractive in my mind. He was tall, had blonde hair and big, blue eyes. He had a gorgeous smile and a sweet tone to his voice. I liked standing next to him in the kitchen while he inspected my work. Sometimes our arms would touch, and I would get a little tingle in my stomach.

Man, he smells good, I thought as I tried to keep focused on the baking instead of on him.

He allowed me to do most of the work as he taught me the techniques to making a good pastry, such as knowing the dough is the right consistency when it hangs off the spatula making a V shape. When the pastries were done, we ate a couple of them and finished the wine. He then gathered his things, thanked me for allowing him to come over, and texted me when he got home.

When I wasn't baking or talking with Mattie, I used the night to practice piano. I had a full-sized electric piano I'd purchased a few years prior. It was nice because I could plug in headphones and play without disturbing the neighbors. I practiced almost every night.

While I tried to occupy my time through the night, it became very difficult to keep up my energy. I was tired all the time. My quality of sleep was greatly diminished. In fact, I had about three hours of quality sleep per night even though I spent anywhere from ten to fourteen hours lying in bed.

This battle with fatigue grew increasingly worse over time. I often cancelled plans because I was so tired I couldn't imagine myself interacting with people, though I craved to be around them. When I cancelled, I felt worse about myself. And thus, the battle with depression grew. I'd always dealt with minor depressive episodes, but they were manageable. However, something changed. It was like my mind, my outlook, and my hope all shifted.

Some of my coworkers moved from nights to days because they were feeling exactly the same way I was. I wanted to switch from nights to days, but there was a dramatic pay decrease and no day positions available. To be honest, I didn't feel like I could afford to move to days, financially. I had to not only afford rent and necessities but also a student loan payment that crippled my income. So I stayed on nights and did my best to handle the discomfort of nocturnal living.

During that time, I started talking to a guy I'd met on one of the dating apps. I don't remember which app, as I had profiles on all of them. He worked as a home health occupational therapist. He was full of kindness and showed he had a heart for people as he chose to go to people's houses to help them with their daily living activities. He was a little bit shorter than me, had a solid build, and was masculine in his mannerisms. We hung out several times, and, more often than not, these times included physical interactions.

I bonded with him every time we hung out but was hindered by my own feelings of inadequacy. I was still traumatized by what had happened in Austin and didn't want to ever play the role of bottom again. With him being a top, I didn't see how we would be compatible sexually. Actually, I wasn't even sure how compatible I would be with any of the guys I was sexually attracted to.

We had planned to go to dinner one evening that I had off. When that day came, I remember hearing the sound of my alarm at 4:00 p.m., signaling me to get up. I let out a moan as the feeling of fatigue crushed me like a ton of bricks. I put my hands on my face and thought, *there is no way I can get up and be social.*

I picked up my phone, squinted at the bright light and texted my friend. "Hey, I'm super sorry for this late message, but I don't think I'm going to be able to meet up tonight. I know it's short notice, but I would love a raincheck." My flakiness offended him, and unfortunately, we never spoke again.

Being a pandemic nurse compounded the already existing issues surrounding health care. While I enjoyed fulfilling a childhood dream, the realities of the job robbed me of the joy I had. Unfortunately, nurses took the brunt of the awful effects of the pandemic. And the coping mechanisms of alcohol and toxic men I used precipitated my mental health decline.

Before long, I no longer found enjoyment in things like baking or playing piano. I just wanted to lie on the couch and do nothing because I felt like I had no energy. But then I felt bad for wasting time. I sat on the couch too tired to move, but also allowed my thoughts to spiral downward, beating myself up that I was lazy.

I knew that I couldn't blame my ongoing depression on just one feeling. I owed my depression to a host of issues. After all, I was still trying to figure out who I was and how I fit into this world. Questions about God and my faith came flooding back into my mind as I wrestled with the reality of this world and where we came from. And these questions usually came to mind when I was most vulnerable trying to stay awake during the dark hours of the night. Who was in control? Why could I not find contentment no matter what I did? Was my dad right when he'd told me that that I wouldn't be happy without God?

I tried to fill the void in my heart with vain things but was left feeling empty. In addition, it is not uncommon for health-care professionals to deal with something called imposter syndrome, and I was no exception. Every day I went into work, I felt inadequate due to my lack of experience and knowledge. As a result, I felt like people were judging me and that the patients had no confidence in me. Every missed IV stick or blood draw or inability to anticipate health outcomes propelled me deeper into the lie that I wasn't enough.

Years of school, countless exams, and certifications are required of a health-care worker. And I might add that hardly any of it actually prepared you for the situations you found yourself in on a daily basis. Everything was constantly changing, and normalcy was a dream. This was how I felt as a novice in the healthcare field. Every day I went into work, I felt as if I was starting over from square one; the more I worked, the more I realized how much I didn't know about medicine and the human body despite long hours of study and passing grades.

Health care felt like a continuous whirlwind that whipped me from moment to moment with no possibility of stabilizing my thoughts or catching my breath. I felt like I was in a paddle boat vigorously rowing toward the shore but the violent tide hurled me back with every forward stroke. I felt like I was walking a tight rope in high winds; I was falling.

So many tasks vied for my attention that the responsibility of staying five steps ahead loomed over me like a giant I couldn't defeat. Work consumed my every thought because when something good was accomplished, fear overrode that excitement. I'd replay the day in my head, *Did I push that IV med too quickly? Did I give the wrong advice? Did I miss a critical lab value? Did I administer the wrong dose? Did the patient lose confidence in me because I missed not one, but two IV placements?* And so on. These questions may seem like trivial complaints, but they haunted my practice.

This lifestyle created a whirlpool of constantly revisiting every action taken, tracing each step, hoping nothing was missed. What an exhausting cycle that grew more powerful with each new day. It was these feelings of anxiety that robbed me of mental and emotional rest.

There was a constant war happening in my mind between doing my best and knowing that I couldn't be perfect. With that, confidence was sacrificed in the crossfire. I felt as if sometimes doing my best wasn't enough, but being perfect wasn't an option. So where was the victory?

When we fail, more likely than not, we spend some time chastising ourselves before we begin to construct a plan to improve the failed skills. The imperative decision is transitioning from chastisement to improvement. Sometimes it is easier to continue punishing ourselves, wallowing in self-pity and getting comfortable by blanketing ourselves with failure, rather than finding a solution. The true test, however, is whether we pick ourselves up to keep learning—and failing.

Learning is a process. And showing up is half the battle.

I think that part of moving forward was celebrating the small victories and not letting the what-if scenarios overcome those victories. I want to share one of those victorious moments with you now. During my first year of nursing, I had a patient who couldn't get out of bed without maximum assistance. A few shifts later, I asked if this patient had any goals while I was with them; they told me that they wanted to lift their legs back into bed without help. I watched as this patient achieved this amazing milestone. On my last shift with that patient, I witnessed them be completely independent. What a miraculous change from the first day. And what a testimony to the results of determination and a will to progress in a healthy way.

As I finished my orientation, I highly underestimated the grueling reality of nursing. I averaged ten thousand steps per day along with a lot of mental and emotional fatigue. I quickly learned that being a nurse was incredibly rewarding, but equivocally exhausting. There was so much to know and so much to do with so little time. The day constantly evolved, which left a choice to either adapt or fall to the side.

I found myself on many occasions asking, *Am I the right person for this job?* I felt like I was hanging on by a very thin thread. At the same time, I felt blessed to have a job during the pandemic and to have people around me who were very kind and supportive through my journey. I knew that I needed to be thankful, but it was difficult when I felt so inadequate.

I talked with Mattie about the challenges we faced as novice nurses. I asked her why it was that we always chose to do the hard things in life.

We realized that it was easy to do easy things; however, it was far more rewarding to do that which was most challenging. If we always did those things that come naturally to us, then there would be no room for growth. I think that everyone wants to excel, but we can't grow from the safety of our comfort zones—growth only happens when we make ourselves vulnerable outside of our safety nets. Being stuck in a routine is comfortable, but it's not rewarding. We need to feel purpose. That purpose is often embedded in difficulty.

I was an anxious mess every time I went into work. I didn't have to be perfect, but I had to be willing. Perfection was unrealistic; while I tried to take my own advice, it was only a matter of time before I met my breaking point.

Even though I kept trying to encourage myself to be positive, there came a point where my mind wouldn't allow myself to see beyond the hollowing feelings that echoed in my soul.

I slowly lost control as I fixated on only the negative things going on in my life. A nasty bot of depression took up residence in my heart and mind rendering me unable to control my emotions. I felt like a black cloud had moved over me so thick that not even the powerful rays of the sun could reach me. I developed fleeting, but recurring, thoughts of letting go of this life. If over the past twenty years I still couldn't find my place in this world, then maybe I didn't have one.

I have a vivid memory of walking along the Chicago River one evening, which was one of my favorite places to be in the city. The area was beautiful, and I admired the buildings as they were strategically placed along the winding waters. At one point, I stopped and looked over the edge with my arms resting on top of the metal bars used as a barrier to keep people from falling into the current. I stared down at the water for a few seconds as I thought about what it might be like to submerge myself. For a few brief moments, it was just the river and me. I suddenly shook myself out of that mental place and continued my walk.

Thoughts about the power of prescription drugs and alcohol entered my mind. What if I mixed them? How would that feel? The curiosity remained locked in my subconscious for months until the thoughts became routine, and action set in. I tried a little bit at a time. I took a Xanax with a cocktail. The feeling was relaxation. I would then fall asleep and wake up rather refreshed the next day. Wow, I actually slept.

One pill and one drink produced a feeling where I could be at peace. For the time being, I remained conservative with the products. I liked to flirt with the idea of losing myself, but my heart reminded me of the small ounce of hope I still had, even though I didn't feel it.

While I was struggling to control my depressive episodes and fleeting thoughts of harming myself, I knew that I needed to try and occupy my time more. I had an interest in medical ethics and knew there was a robust ethics program at Northwestern. I reached out to the medical ethics advisors at Northwestern and set up a meeting to discuss potential involvement. After the meeting, we both felt it was right to have me join an extracurricular program called being a medical ethics resource nurse. With this, I'd start the orientation process which was held online consisting of zoom meetings and small projects to help gain more knowledge of medical ethics and how to deal with certain situations.

I enjoyed what I was learning and being a part of this team. One of the medical ethics advisors told me about a program offered at the university, a master of bioethics. Working at the hospital granted me a small scholarship, so I applied to the program. I was also offered to sit in on one course to get a feel for what the program would be like. The course was intro to medical ethics. We read about and discussed many cases during the class. My interest was piqued, and I looked forward to the class each week.

Around this time, I met a guy online who took my breath away. He was a travel nurse making quadruple the amount of money as me. He was about five nine, with light-brown skin and an athletic build that made it apparent he spent time at the gym working out. He caught my eye on Grindr, but he sent the first message. He flattered me with words, saying how he loved my eyes, and he liked that I was also a nurse. He'd tell me about his travel nursing experiences and share details about negotiating his contracts to get the money he felt like he deserved. And with the pandemic ravaging the world, those negotiated contracts were usually honored.

His flattery, coupled with his undeniably good looks, captured my heart. After messaging back and forth for a few days, we opted to meet out at a restaurant in downtown Chicago. We met one night after my ethics class and walked over to the restaurant. He was even more gorgeous in person than his photos. I felt nervous and a bit intimidated, wondering what a guy like that saw in me.

As we talked through dinner, I could tell that we weren't a match because our goals and outlooks on life didn't match. He wanted an open relationship, spent days off doing drugs, and going to raves and invited me to join him. I told him I wasn't into that scene, which was difficult to say because I wanted him to like me. I was so enthralled with his body and physique that I made myself believe we were the perfect match. And he stayed interested, so I looked forward to each day spent with him.

Our first night together was electric. The way he kissed me and touched me made me feel like nothing else mattered in the world. And all I wanted was more. I told him that I liked him, and he told me the same. In the back of my mind, thoughts of anxiety brewed as I thought about our sexual compatibility. *Would he take me with my condition?* I wondered. *Would I be forced into another situation I don't want to be in?* I kept these thoughts to myself but they echoed in my mind every time we met.

I shared with him my thoughts about wanting to become a nurse practitioner and getting more involved with medical ethics. He listened as I spoke about my dreams, but he asked me why I would want to do all of those things when I could make way more money staying as a bedside nurse, especially if I started to travel. He said it was a lot of work, school, and money to get those degrees, and the payoff would be little. I enjoyed learning, and the goals I set for myself made me more excited for future prospects, but what he said made sense, and I felt foolish for wanting to enhance myself in that way if the return wouldn't be worth it. Why would I spend all that time and money studying when I could be making so much more as a bedside nurse working three days a week? Instead of pushing me forward toward my goals, I let him talk me out of fulfilling them.

I became jealous of him and his travel-nurse experiences. He was living a stress-free life, making more money and partying. In comparison, I was overworking myself and feeling severely underpaid as I was living paycheck to paycheck. I felt inferior and inadequate, allowing my depression to take hold of these areas.

He dominated my thoughts and feelings. I was enthralled with his sexual energy, and he continued to flatter me with his affirming words. We hung out often; we took long walks on the beach, went out for cocktails, shared boba tea, and snuggled on the couch while watching *RuPaul's Drag Race* or *Real Housewives of Atlanta*. Like a couple but without the label, we held hands as we walked down the street and shared a kiss or two at a crosswalk as we waited for that little white man to light up. I craved the attention he gave me, and I fought through my tiredness to be with him.

One evening as we were on the couch watching TV, we talked about working out, and he brought up the idea of going to a circuit party, an all-night dancing event where people normally show up in skimpy costumes. I told him that I didn't feel comfortable accompanying him to one, and I really didn't like him going because I knew that those events often included people engaging in sexual activities while being high on drugs. But he expressed that he wanted to be free and open.

He then lifted up my shirt and asked, "So, do you want to go to the gym, then?"

Immediately embarrassed, I pulled my shirt down quickly and said, "I don't mind the idea of going to the gym, but I have been lacking the motivation."

He said OK, and I told him that it was time I went home.

That conversation imprinted on my mind. A few days later, he then told me that he didn't think things were working out for us. He wanted someone with a better build, someone who wanted to be more open sexually, and someone with whom he could do the things he enjoyed.

Even though I knew we were wrong for each other, I was distraught when he told me the reasons that he didn't want to be with me. He'd attacked my person, my body. And I once again felt like I wasn't good enough for people. But I decided to make a change.

Chapter Twenty Eight

I knew that I wasn't where I wanted to be. I'm a firm believer that if you're unhappy with where you are, then change it. We all have the opportunity to make a better life for ourselves, but the scary part is actually doing it. I knew that I needed to make a change. In fact, I wanted to get out of Chicago. But I felt trapped. I wanted a new start, but I didn't know how to make it happen. And I didn't believe I had the gumption to make change a reality. I was barely making ends meet. My stress and anxiety grew because I didn't see a way out.

Around that time, I had my one-year quality meeting with my manager on the transplant unit. During the meeting, we talked about my performance over the past year. I was relieved to know that I was on track and my manager was happy with how I was doing at work. We also discussed future plans. I told her that I was unhappy. We chatted about night shift taking a serious toll on me and that I was becoming uncontrollably depressed. We determined that it was time for me to move on to something else. I felt a little bit of hope glimmer in my heart as a result of our conversation. I breathed a sigh of relief, and I thought, *there is something more. I can move on from this.*

The ICU had always interested me, and I thought that ICU nursing would give me what I was looking for as far as implementing more responsibility within the scope of my practice. My manager was very supportive and helped me with the transition. She set up a shadow in the neuro-spine ICU, which was my first choice. I interviewed and, a few weeks later, joined their team. It was bittersweet to be leaving my family on the transplant unit. But the critical care environment offered an exciting new start.

The ICU was exhilarating. It was busy. And there was a lot of new information to learn. This environment didn't help my imposter syndrome, but it allowed me to develop my skills and widened my scope of practice.

As part of my orientation, I was enrolled in several critical care classes and skills labs that I attended on my days off. The information we talked about was exciting, and I wanted to learn; however, I hit an emotional wall again. My sleep was horribly disturbed as I was frequently startled awake, worrying I'd forgotten to do something or did something incorrectly at work.

The difficulties surrounding nursing coupled with lack of acceptance from my family and the internal war I continued to have with my faith against my sexual identity built up into a colossal explosion. I felt sad and would burst into tears for no reason. One night I was making meatballs, and as I was mixing the beef and spices together with my hands, I just started crying uncontrollably. These meatballs weren't that bad; why was I crying over them? An aloneness crowded me and isolated me to the point where I didn't want to go out or hang out with friends. Instead, I sat on my kitchen floor, drank tequila and assuaged my anxiety with a pill or two until I gently fell asleep.

I tried reading self-help books; I tried writing; I tried meditation and yoga; I even tried deflecting from my own problems by helping others with theirs. Nothing seemed to work. I thought about calling my parents and asking for advice, but I knew they would redirect me to the Bible and relegate all these unwanted feelings to being gay. I couldn't have that battle.

In an effort to calm my spirit, I often went across the street to sit by the lake to think. I would bring a big picnic blanket and lay it over the plush green grass under the shade of a gigantic tree. I would sit there gazing at the horizon, which seemed to have no end. Would I ever find my purpose?

Sadness, loneliness, and hopelessness controlled me. I felt powerless under their spell, and unless you've been through that kind of debilitating depression, it's hard to imagine or understand the impact it has. I actually posted about feeling depressed on social media and someone replied by saying that I just needed to choose to be happy—as if it were that simple.

Usually, I could give myself a pep talk and snap out of it, but this time it was different. It was a lingering void that grew bigger and deeper with every breath I took. I spent hours lying on the floor staring at the wall, feeling absolutely lifeless.

One particular day at work, I had a routine meeting with the education coordinator, Andrea, on my unit. I enjoyed these meetings because they allowed me to build a professional relationship with the manager and the education coordinator, and they allowed me to speak about what was and wasn't going well as I transitioned into this new role. During this get-together, Andrea looked at me and asked in a genuine tone, "Are you OK? You don't seem like your normal, chipper self."

She always had a calm and welcoming presence; I felt comfortable with her. I paused and looked at her for a few seconds before I answered. All I wanted to do was cry, but I held back the tears as I said, "I'm fine, just dealing with a lot of personal stuff."

She looked at me with caring eyes. "If you need anything at all, please know that I'm here to talk. And I mean that as a friend, not one of your superiors."

I knew she meant it. And I desired so badly to pour out my heart to her because I knew she would listen with a loving ear and a tender heart. But I had no clue how to even begin to articulate the overwhelming sense of depression and anxiety that I was dealing with. It was really something out of my control. I felt as if I was just existing in a pool of emotions while I went through the motions. I also wanted to continue the facade that I had everything together. I didn't want her to think that I was weak or that I was failing. Just like when I was growing up, I wanted to be the best. I didn't want people to know I had problems. I wanted praise for a job well done, not pity. But I was breaking inside.

I remember one particularly difficult day at work I standing in front of the Omnicell (medication dispenser) getting ready to pull medications, feeling dazed by all the tasks I had to do. I started thinking how easy it would be to just take a bunch of my Xanax with a glass of wine and peacefully let myself go. I pondered the sweet bliss of allowing my mind and body to become numb from all the frustration and anxiety I was feeling. I quickly came back to my senses, pulled out the necessary meds for my patient and got to work.

After I finished giving report that day, a coworker looked at me and said, "It seems like something is wrong. Is everything OK?"

"I feel overwhelmed," I replied.

She said in a caring, sweet tone, "There is a lot to learn in the ICU, much is expected of us. But with time, it'll get easier and you will be astounded by your progress."

I knew she was right, but I felt like the process between how I was doing now and "easier" was undoable. I lost faith in myself. I lost hope. And without hope, I lost purpose. And without purpose, I lost my intent to live.

After that shift, I had two days off, and then I would be back working three days in a row, one of the days being Thanksgiving. I clocked out and, little did I know, that time would be the last.

Chapter Twenty Nine

The following day was November 20. I woke up with a little extra spring in my step because I'd made plans with my close friend and coworker, Elyse, from the transplant unit to visit the Christmas market in downtown. This was a tradition that I loved.

We planned to meet at the market around 7:00 p.m. This was the first weekend that the market opened, so it was very crowded. We stood in line for a while before we were able to enter. We walked around and visited all of the shops admiring the art and fancy Christmas decorations as we drank hot chocolate from that year's signature Christkindle mug.

When we finished perusing the market, Elyse mentioned that she had a birthday party to go to. I was bummed when she told me she had other plans as I was wanting to continue the evening together, especially since we weren't working together anymore. But I told her that it was totally fine and that I would probably hit up a gay bar closer to home; however, I knew in my mind that I wouldn't do that. I felt too self-conscious going to bars alone. So I went home feeling sad that we couldn't hang out more.

When I arrived home, I took out my cocktail shaker and began to make a drink. I figured that if I was going to be alone, then I would just drink myself into oblivion. I remember texting with a friend who extended an invitation to come over to his place, but I wasn't in the mood to hook up. I wanted a friend, not a sexual invite for the night. I told him that I was feeling sad and that I opted to drink my feelings. He told me that he preferred that I come over to his place to cuddle so I didn't have to be alone. While the gesture was nice, I knew what that meant, and I wasn't going to fall for that trap this time.

I continued drinking and, with each drink, my mind slowly unraveled. The thoughts of taking a Xanax and Norco came rushing back into my mind dressed up as a good time and a sweet release from all of the hurt I'd been feeling. I'd thought about it for so long, and now I felt like it was time to give it a try.

I confidently walked into the bathroom where I knew the stash was. I opened the mirror and saw those little orange pill bottles I'd been saving. I stared at those bottles and let the thoughts sink in before I grabbed them and walked back to the kitchen.

I turned on my hip-hop playlist and created my own vibes as I bopped to the music, throwing back cocktails while I rearranged the pills on the counter. I let my thoughts go. I put a pill in my mouth and washed it down with a shot of tequila in between the glasses of Chardonnay I had poured. I think at one point, I just drank from the bottle. As I kept the routine going, my mind became numb. My feelings were paralyzed, and I thought of nothing except for what was right in front of me.

All of the negative feelings I have ever felt came rushing back to me. My feelings of inadequacy, my hatred of being gay, my desire for my family's acceptance, my feelings of aloneness, depression, anxiety, stress, hopelessness, lostness, struggle, defeat, never feeling like I was enough bombarded me.

I was beaten and tortured by my own thoughts of self-doubt. I simply stopped believing in myself, and I had nothing left to live for. In those moments, I felt like I went into auto-pilot. My brain took control of both my actions and my reasoning. A plan was set into motion, and there was no turning back because I relinquished control.

For the second time, my life erupted, like a bombshell but this time the effects went deeper.

I continued drinking and took a few more pills. I then grabbed my phone and began composing a text to my family that was sent at 4:26 a.m.

It read:

I love you all very much. A few thoughts:

I want to assist each of the kids with their college funds from what I have to my name.

I'm so sorry for any pain or disappointment I've caused. I didn't ask for it and neither did you. Yet it's the reality of our story. I want to stop the hurt.

I never quite hit the mark, but I'm hoping and trusting that God will have mercy on me. He created a miserable life for me, but I still trust in his sovereignty. Although he's all-powerful, my strength is in vain. I have nothing left. I wanted to be great, but the weight of loneliness has won over my will.

I have never been able to find my place in this world. I'm too different. Being gay is the most torturous of human existences.

I have been between a rock and a hard place for the better half of my life. It's caught up with me. I want to be free. Freedom.

I love you.

I passed out on the kitchen floor.

Hours later, I somehow woke up to the sound of my phone ringing. The caller ID said "Unknown." I usually keep my phone on silent or vibrate, but for some reason, I had it on loud volume, and I'm glad I did.

While I was barely clinging to consciousness, I answered the phone as I lay face down on the kitchen floor. I hit the green circle to accept the call and said in a mumbled voice, "Hello?"

I heard a woman's voice speaking to me. A voice that was strong and serious, yet caring and genuine. I wasn't even sure how she'd gotten my number. But the conversation went a little something like this:

"Jordan? Is that you?"

I said, "Yes. Who is this?"

"This is 911," she said and stated her name. "A lot of people are worried about you. Can you tell me what's going on?"

I burst into tears, screaming, "I'm all alone, and nobody wants me!"

"That is not true," she replied. "Many people are worried about you."

"I just want it to stop," I told her.

"Jordan, an ambulance is outside of your house right now. Can you let them in?"

"There is no one here! Don't lie!" I exclaimed.

The truth is that I'd recently moved, and the address on file for me was my old apartment.

With urgency in her voice, she asked, "Jordan, can you tell me your new address?"

"I don't know you. I don't know you're you!" I said between tearful sobs.

She stated her name. "I want to help you, Jordan. You have so much to live for, and many people want to help you."

"If they wanted me, then they wouldn't make me feel so miserable. I want out."

"We are here for you, Jordan, and I know that you're hurting, but there is more you can live for than what you're currently feeling. Would you be willing to tell me your new address?"

"I'm going to take more pills," I told her.

"Jordan, please don't take any more pills," the dispatcher begged.

I eventually told her my address.

"Jordan, thank you! The paramedics are on their way," she said.

Then, in a very clear and direct tone, she instructed, "Jordan, I need you to get up, unlock the door, and wait on the phone with me for the paramedics to arrive."

I listened to her. With haste and determination, I got up, stumbled to the door, unlocked it, and crawled back to the kitchen, put my face to the phone that was on the floor and said, "Okay, I did it."

"Great, Jordan! The paramedics are only a few minutes away. Stay on the phone with me, OK?"

I told her that I was going to finish off the pills. Again, she begged me not to. I remember grabbing for the bottle in hopes I could ingest a few more tablets before the paramedics arrived. I don't remember if I did.

I began to fall back asleep just as I heard a pounding at my door. The paramedics entered in haste and found me on the kitchen floor. I was limp, unable to open my eyes and felt like I was falling into a deep sleep, but I could still hear.

As the paramedics approached me, I heard one of them say in a harsh and judgmental tone, "Get up! Stop trying to kill yourself." Those were the last words I heard before I passed out again and fell into a deep sleep.

I arrived at the emergency department of a nearby hospital (not where I worked) around 6:50 a.m., which, upon reflection, was when nurses changed shifts, so it wasn't great timing.

The nurses immediately placed me on oxygen, inserted three IVs in my left arm, and hooked me up to the heart monitor. My blood pressure was dangerously low and the medication I took relaxed my body and breathing muscles. I was given four liters of fluid to help regulate my blood pressure. As my blood pressure lowered, my heart rate increased to compensate for the lack of blood distribution throughout my body. My breathing then became compromised. I was now taking eight breaths per minute. Normal breaths per minute is between twelve and twenty for a healthy adult. As a result of the decreased breathing, my breaths were shallow and infrequent. I was placed on an oxygen mask while the critical care team was called because of my deterioration. I was admitted to the ICU for respiratory depression, but there were no beds available at that time. So I stayed in the ED until an ICU bed became available.

Angel, our family friend, was still living in Chicago. My dad had immediately called her and told her of the situation. Out of abundance of kindness, she'd provided my parents and sister flights from their houses to Chicago to be with me.

My sister-in-law had been the first one to see the text I'd sent to the family chain. She'd woken up early in the morning unexpectedly, looked at her phone, and seen what I'd sent. She'd then made calls to my other family members in hopes of putting some pieces together. But everyone had been as surprised as she was. My dad had immediately called Angel, who'd called the Chicago fire department. My sister-in-law had gone through my Instagram posts from the previous night. I'd tagged Elyse at the Christmas market that night. So my sister-in-law called her to see if she knew of anything, but unfortunately, she hadn't had any information to share. Elyse had called a few of our other friends to try and gather any insight into what was happening. And she, along with some of my friends and coworkers, had called my phone several times.

My family scrambled around figuring out how to best handle the situation. My sister decided to be the first to rush to Chicago. That morning she unexpectedly left a newborn, two young kids, and her husband and drove from Charleston to Cleveland, where she got on the next flight to Chicago. Angel met her at the airport and drove herself straight to the hospital where I was.

Because of COVID, visiting rules were very strict. But as soon as the nurses heard one of my family members had arrived, they immediately escorted her to the bedside because of the severity of my condition.

Before coming to the bedside, the nurse told my sister that the situation didn't look good. As my sister joined me at the bedside, my condition waxed and waned. My vital signs were in a ping-pong match as my body fought against the chemical reaction of the combination of pills and alcohol I'd consumed. As my life hung in the balance, the question of whether to intubate remained on the table.

The ED doctors wanted to intubate given my severe respiratory depression, low blood pressure, and now my new onset respiratory acidosis, which is an accumulation of carbon dioxide from a lack of ventilation. My two nurses, however, looked at the situation as a whole, weighing the outcomes of intubating and not intubating. Their intuition and experience suggested against intubation. They wanted to give me my best chance at fighting, and placing me on a machine would take that power away. This battle went on for several hours as my status fluctuated to and from dangerous levels. But I somehow pulled through. When we were able to flush my system of the narcotics and benzodiazepines, my breathing returned. The treatment team were grateful they had decided not to intubate.

After the fact, my sister told me that my nurses were amazing. She said that one nurse pulled up a chair and stayed by my side her entire shift for close monitoring and immediate intervention as I greeted death during those critical hours. My sister also told me that my nurse had stayed after her shift to ensure I was OK and that my family had the support they needed. That right there is nursing in a nutshell.

My parents and my middle brother arrived a few hours after my sister. They were getting caught up with my condition and next steps. An ICU bed still was unavailable. The social worker decided for me to be moved to an inpatient psych hospital for evaluation and stabilization due to my significant suicide attempt and emotional instability. My dad, being a therapist, requested that I be released into his care. The team explained that since the paperwork was already sent and approved for my transfer and admission, it couldn't be undone. There would be no way for my dad to assume care.

I spent the night in the ED. Early Monday morning, I was transferred to an inpatient psych hospital. I have no recollection of my time in the ED. Even currently, I have only one single memory between my interaction with EMS and waking up days later in an inpatient facility. I have the faintest memory of the time I was being transferred. While in the ambulance, I looked over and muttered the words, "I have made a terrible mistake." Then lost consciousness once again. I don't know if that was a true memory or a dream, but it is the only recollection I have. And an insightful one.

Chapter Thirty

Monday

I arrived early at the facility if which I have no recollection of. I slept through the day and night as the drugs wore off.

Tuesday

I woke up to the sound of a man's voice kindly saying, "It's seven o'clock. Time to get ready for breakfast."

I opened my eyes and guessed we were about the same age. He was about my height, had short, dirty-blond hair, and a scruffy beard. As he made his way to the bathroom, I halfway sat up in my bed studying my unfamiliar surroundings. Where was I? I lifted the weight of five hospital blankets off of me and slowly turned until my feet hit the floor. I looked down, and I saw I was wearing nonskid hospital socks. As I stood up, I lightly touched the edge of the bed to keep my balance, noticing the flutter of my hospital gown. Where were my clothes? I walked toward the door and looked down the long well-lit hallway.

Unaware of where I was, I passed people in the hall as they greeted me by saying, "Good morning, Jordan!"

Who were these people? And how did they know my name?

At the end of the hallway, there was a nurse standing behind a counter handing out medications to people standing in line. As I walked a bit further, I passed by the nurses' station and then arrived at a bigger room.

Straight ahead there were double doors. To the right was a single door that led to a room the size of a small classroom. As I looked to the back of the room, I noticed two square tables each with four wooden chairs. And to my left, there were several chairs facing a small TV that was mounted on the wall. It looked like something you would see in a doctor's office waiting area.

I sat down in one of the chairs next to someone I didn't know. People were chatting with one another and watching the television. I sat there for a few minutes before I got back up and slowly made my way back to my room. I lay down in my bed, pulled the heavy blankets over me, and closed my eyes.

Tuesday, I woke up to the sound of people walking through the hall-way outside of my room. I looked out the window, and it was light out-side. I slowly got up and walked down the hall to the dayroom where people greeted me by my name. I still had no idea who these people were. I finally asked someone, "What day is it?"

They kindly replied, "It's Tuesday."

Tuesday! I thought. *How on earth is it Tuesday?* The last memory I had was that it was Saturday. I leaned back in my chair in disbelief.

Not long after, one of the staff nurses handed me a paper box and told me that they had saved me some lunch. I nodded and opened the box. Apparently, lunch had been hamburger and fries, which had been sitting out for a while because it was cold. I bit into one of the stale fries, then closed the box and threw it away.

About that time, I heard my name called. I looked up and saw a nicely dressed man waving at me to come over. He introduced himself as the director of nursing at the facility and wanted to let me know that he had spoken with my dad and my family. He said that they pleaded for my release. But because of my "serious attempt," the facility wouldn't allow for an immediate discharge. Normally, they kept people like me for a minimum of ten days, but he told me that they would try to cut back on my time in the facility. I told him with a desperate voice that I wasn't trying to kill myself and begged for them to let me go with my family. The answer was no.

I stood in front of him in my hospital gown, speechless. I kept repeating to him that I wasn't trying to die. He reiterated that he would speak with the other directors about my early discharge.

Toward the end of our conversation, one of the other staff members came up behind me and wrapped the gown tighter around me and said, "Whoops, you were hanging out."

"Thank you," I replied. And they told me my clothes should be coming up from security in a few hours. Now I knew how my patients felt walking around with their backsides hanging out. As a nurse, I'd never paid attention to it, but as the patient, it was embarrassing.

A couple of hours later, I met with my social worker. We sat at a table in a cold room, and she opened up her computer and proceeded to ask me questions about what had happened. I told her that I really didn't know. I was so confused by everything that had occurred in the last seventy-two hours and still trying to get my bearings about where I even was. My mind was foggy, and my speech was slow and slurred. I tried to recall what had happened, but I kept telling her I wasn't trying to kill myself.

She told me that I had a pretty significant attempt to take my life. But I kept telling her that I wasn't trying to die. I told her that I was a nurse and if I really wanted to die then I would have made it happen. I told her that I knew how many pills I could take before respiratory failure and that I didn't get to that point.

She looked at me with a very serious look and said, "Well, the hospital staff is saying that you had a very serious attempt. We talked with the nurses and physicians at the hospital and they were all very worried for you." She told me that they'd almost intubated me in the ED. I told her that it wasn't an attempt.

We played this back and forth for a few minutes, and then I asked her when I could leave. She told me that the usual length of stay for suicide attempts was seven-to-ten days, but since this was my first attempt and that it was significant, they tended to extend the stay for safety (and, of course, liability).

I said, "Please no!" I ensured her that I will be safe with my family. She stood up, walked toward the door while saying that she would request for a seven-day detainment, and that it would start today.

We were given phone time twice a day—once in the afternoon between 12:00 and 1:00 p.m. and once in the evening between 6:00 p.m. and 7:00 p.m. That Tuesday night, I received a phone call from my family. I don't recall with whom I spoke first, but I remember it was a difficult conversation. All I could do was cry. I fought back tears as I spoke and barely spoke a sentence before I would have to stop, breathe, and relax myself unless I burst into tears. I felt so distant from those who were familiar to me. All I wanted was to be within the safe boundaries of my family.

I remember my sister talking to me with a very calm but hopeful voice. She was a rock that anchored my weary soul during those desolate days. On that Tuesday night she told me that she and my dad were working very hard to get me out of there as soon as possible. She told me that they sat in the hospital lobby all day Monday until someone came to speak with them about what was going on; they were working on getting me out on Wednesday, and they had been praying that I would have a good support team while I was there. The receptionist at the hospital told my family that that Raquel, my social worker, was her favorite. She told me that my nurse went and spoke with them about my care, which encouraged them a lot. And they said that they were impressed with how the director was handling everything. She was encouraged that God was answering her prayers, and reminded me that I would be OK.

Even though I felt like I was broken into a million pieces, her words helped me feel whole. The phone was passed to my mom, and she asked if she could read a few verses from the Bible. I said yes, and as she read a few comforting passages from the Psalms, I cried silently as I hunched over in my seat and pressed the phone firmly against my ear to try to get closer to the comfort of my mom's voice. The phone call came to an end, and as I hung up the phone, I felt a horrible disconnect. I was trapped behind locked doors, and there was nothing I could do about it. I was distraught. I had absolutely nothing left.

I got up from where I'd been seated to take the phone call and went over to the nurses' station. I asked one of the nurses if there was any way I could get ahold of the health records from the hospital ED so I could look at them. A few minutes later, the nurse walked over to where I was sitting in the dayroom and handed me a piece of paper he had printed. He told me that he wasn't able to get a full record, but was able to get a short report for my admission to the psych hospital. I looked at the paper and began to read the note.

"31yo white male presented to Weiss ED via EMS for SI attempt OD on Xanax/norco/alcohol. Pt reports he wants to 'forget my life' because 'It's all too much.' Pt reports he is all alone & has no friends or family. Pt reports hx of anxiety. Pt reports he wants to stop the pain of existing. Pt couldn't stop crying. Pt is unable to contract for safety and needs inpatient hospitalization for safety and stabilization."

Another note read, "Pt was brought to ED via EMS after intentionally overdosing on 37 xanax, 10 norco and alcohol. Pt admits to taking 20 Xanax at 1 a.m. 17 xanax at 5am and 10 Norco during the time in between to 'take away the pain.' Pt minimized sx while at the ED and wouldn't provide any details that led up to the suicide attempt. Pt does admit to feeling overwhelmed and depressed since he started working as a nurse at NMH. Pt endorses depressive sx, panic attacks, social isolation, hopelessness, helplessness, poor concentration, sleep disturbance and anhedonia. Pt is in need of immediate hospitalization for safety and stabilization. 11/22/21 0710"

I looked at the nurse, who looked back at me with a serious expression as he told me I was in pretty bad shape. I told him that I wasn't trying to kill myself. Before heading back to my room, the nurse gave me a notebook and a marker for journaling. They wouldn't give out pencils or pens. I walked back to my room, brushed my teeth with the toiletries that were provided to us, and climbed into bed. I sang hymns like "How Great Thou Art" and "Great Is Thy Faithfulness" in my head as I tried to fall asleep.

Wednesday

The next day I woke up feeling more coherent about my surroundings, though still very uncomfortable with where I found myself. I got up and sat on the edge of my bed as I rubbed my eyes looking for any amount of strength to stand up and walk out into the hall. Once again, my roommate invited me to join everyone at breakfast. His spirit was gentle, and his presence was calming. I passed people standing in line to get their morning meds as I made my way into the dayroom. I sat myself down in a padded chair and watched the news playing on the TV.

People of all colors and ethnicities occupied the halls of that psych hospital. I was surprised at how many older people were there. I don't know what they were there for, but something told me by the way they carried themselves that this wasn't their first admittance to the hospital. I also noticed many people who identified as gender nonbinary, trans, and/or gay. I heard stories told by patients how their families abandoned them or abused them. I saw a great deal of hurt and tremendous emotional burdens carried by these people from the environments from which they came. These people around me searched for love and fulfillment in relationships, drugs, and alcohol, which all left them empty. Their struggles really weren't much different than yours or mine; it just so happened that their habits caught up with them, like they did mine. No one is exempt from finding themselves inside the walls of a psych hospital.

At breakfast, I barely took two bites of the rubbery waffles. I made sure to stay away from the liquid eggs they poured onto the skillet from a cardboard container, and the meat didn't entice me. I didn't have a big appetite anyway. I just wanted to go home. I looked around for the director to see if he had any word on my discharge, which I hoped might be today. I saw him walk into the cafeteria as we were all lining up. I walked over to him and asked about my discharge. He told me that he had spoken with my dad about leaving today, but the other people in his committee were not willing to sign off on my early discharge. He gave me a serious look and said that he would try for Friday, but they were leaning toward Monday. Hearing those words, I thought I might have died again. My heart sank even deeper into the abyss. Where was my hope now?

After breakfast, we made our way back to our unit. I sat in the same chair as before and stared up at the TV.

How am I ever going to survive this? I thought. I looked around for inspiration for how I might occupy my time. I knew I couldn't physically escape, but I could mentally escape. And what better way to do that than to immerse myself in a story? I immediately walked over to the nurses' station and asked if there were any books I could read. The nurse happily gave me a stack of books that I began to sift through. I decided that I might read *The Strange Case of Dr. Jekyll and Mr. Hyde*. I loved the musical, so I knew I might like the book as well. I took it back to my seat in the dayroom and opened to the first page. I began reading; I teleported myself to the Victorian era in London, embracing the mysterious lives of Dr. Jekyll, Mr. Hyde, Lucy, and Emma. I read for hours, no longer noticing the painful ticks of the clock, which made it seem as if time stood still.

Twice a day, a social worker came in to conduct a group activity. These activities were not mandatory, but attendance helped shorten one's length of stay because it showed participation and desire to help yourself. I attended every meeting.

During that first session, we were given sand art to create with. It was Thanksgiving time, so the social worker handed out pieces of paper with Thanksgiving-themed pictures. We could take the tape off of the picture and fill in the sticky parts with whichever color of sand we chose. I'm not at all creative, so my final product looked as if it had been completed by a six-year-old, but I didn't care. I carefully sprinkled the colored sand over the picture and dusted it off so that only the sand that stuck to the paper remained. I repeated this with a variety of colors until I was done. As I scattered the sand across the piece of art, I remember feeling just like the sand that stuck to the paper. I was stuck. I felt so alone that it was often hard to breathe. I felt like a toddler, helpless and constantly being watched by staff workers. The activity helped pass the time, but it didn't help to abate the horrible burden of emptiness I felt inside.

After the meeting, I immediately went back to reading. I sat, knees to chest, in the chair, invested in the lives of these characters I made come alive in my mind. It was all I could do to survive.

During a phone call that day, I asked about my job and immediately stressed about missing work. My family reassured me that they had spoken with my manager already and that it was taken care of for now. There was nothing I needed to worry about. I, then, talked to my sister, and she told me that the family had talked and thought it would be best for me to move away from Chicago. She told me that when I got discharged, she would take me home with her, and I would live there.

I said, "Okay."

She asked me if I understood and I said, "Yes." So she said that they would pack up my stuff in my apartment and start planning for me to move in with her. I remember feeling very overwhelmed by all that was happening, but I also didn't have the decisional capacity to think through what was being asked of me. At that moment, all I wanted to do was be with my family. I didn't comprehend what I'd agreed to, but I didn't care. I just wanted to be out of that place.

That day, my roommate was discharged. I remember being so jealous of him as he gathered his things and walked out the door into freedom. He was very nice and polite to me. I hated to see him go, but wished even more that it was me. However, even in the midst of my complete brokenness, I knew that the day would come when I would walk out those doors. I knew that soon my family would be waiting for me. And I pictured myself walking through those doors and running toward my family, never looking back at this place again. I thought about that image constantly which provided me hope to hold on one more day.

That night, I relaxed a little bit as my old roommate's bed was left unoccupied. I knew at some point the bed would be filled with an admission, but for that moment, I felt like I could breathe a little more comfortably. By nature, I'm a very private person, and I need my space. Having to share a room and a bathroom with a complete stranger was a little more than unnerving for me.

My private bliss didn't last long. In the middle of the night, I was awoken by the staff getting a new patient settled into the room. I let out a moan and hoped to God that this new roommate wouldn't be a problem.

Thursday

On Thanksgiving Day of 2021, I woke up around 7:00 a.m. and started my normal routine of sitting up in bed, brushing my fingers through my hair, and grabbing my book before walking out into the hall to wait for breakfast. Every morning, I entered the dayroom, sat in the same chair, and opened my book to begin reading where I'd last left off. The days were all exactly the same. The routine was monotonous. The repetitive motions were mind-numbing. I felt like a robot following commands and staying in line.

That Thanksgiving is one I will never forget. That day wasn't filled with family, fun, laughter, and food. I continued with the mundane activities and counted down the days until I would be discharged. And there was still a small speckle of hope in my heart that tomorrow, Friday, would be my discharge.

That afternoon I received my regular phone call from my sister and family. On that phone call, my sister explained to me how things were going with the packing and moving. She discussed with me that if I wasn't able to be discharged tomorrow, then she and my brother would travel back to her house with my stuff and then come back to Chicago over the weekend to pick me up on Monday.

I replied with a surprised and broken, "You're leaving me?"

And she immediately and firmly reassured me saying, "No, I'm not leaving. We were just thinking it might be easier to drop your stuff off at my house and then come back to get you."

Not understanding I replied, "You're leaving?"

She replied, "Jordan, I would never leave if I thought that I couldn't get back to you. I can be on a plane and be back to Chicago in three hours. I'm *not* leaving you."

After a moment of silence, I agreed it would be OK. And I knew my sister needed to get back to her two young children and ten-month-old baby. And deep down, I knew she would be back.

During my time there, word got out that I was a nurse. I'm not sure how people knew, but I'm assuming staff knew and passed it along by word of mouth. I didn't talk about it, but it seemed like everyone knew. Even during our meetings, sometimes the staff member conducting the meeting would bring up the fact that I was a nurse. I didn't mind that people knew, but it did make me feel a little bit uncomfortable as I was a nurse, yet a patient in a psych unit. I remember, during one of the meetings, my nursing background was brought up, and a fellow patient asked how I could be a patient there if I was a nurse. A bit stunned, I looked at him, then I looked at the staff member, back at the patient who made the comment, and said, "Well, we need help too sometimes."

Every day, our vitals were taken once in the morning and once in the evening. I remember one evening a tech was taking vitals, and she told me how nervous she was to take my vitals because I was nurse. She said that she was new and not used to taking vitals. I told her to relax and that it wasn't a big deal.

She said, "I know, but you're a nurse."

And I said, "Yep, and I'm the one sitting in this chair, and you're not."

I felt like, even though I was a patient, knowing I was a nurse, they held me to a higher standard. I almost felt like there was a pressure there to be better and to know better. The more that word got out of my health-care background, the more patients started to ask me questions about health-care needs they had and medications they were taking. I was more than happy to discuss these things with people, but this wasn't the setting. I was in no place to be giving medical advice to people at that time. I listened to them, and kindly redirected them to speak with their health-care provider or the nurses who were on duty at the hospital. I did enjoy talking with others about their health. It made me feel important and helped me feel good about helping others even when I was at my lowest.

There were two staff members who stood out to me. The first was a nurse. The first night that I remember when I was there, he asked me if I would like anything to help me sleep. He acted very surprised when I responded with a "No, thank you." I guess most people request sleeping agents.

He worked the night shift, and I saw him a few different times that week. He was always so kind in his words and treated me with such compassion. I remember one conversation we had about working as a nurse. He told me it must have been difficult working in the ICU to which I affirmed. He encouraged me to take a trip. He kept telling me to travel, take a trip, and relax. His words warmed my spirit.

The other staff member I want to mention is one of the techs who I interacted with on many occasions. She was very easy to talk with and showed a genuine interest in getting to know all of us. I could tell she cared. Her presence was comforting and her words were affirming. Later that week, she told me that she was on duty when I'd arrived at the unit.

She told me that I was so out of it that she was concerned that my acuity wasn't appropriate for that floor. I could barely stand on my own. She told me that she'd sat me down at one of the tables in the dayroom to eat a lunch they had saved, but I'd fallen asleep face down on the table.

I was embarrassed by my behavior as she described my beginning days there, but she acted as if everything was normal. There was no judgment. She was happy to help and attentive to my needs during those moments. I will never forget her kindness.

Friday

At last, Friday came. That morning, though, I had a few butterflies in my stomach as I hoped and wished and prayed for my discharge. I didn't know what was going to happen, but I was remaining optimistic.

After breakfast, I found the director of nursing once again and asked about my possible discharge. He told me in his usual tone they wouldn't allow my early departure. He said they might try for Saturday, but most likely it'd be Monday. My heart sank, and I felt my entire body sag like a thousand-pound weight landed on my shoulders. I walked back to my seat, opened my book, and buried myself in a world much better than the reality that currently surrounded me.

My new roommate was an absolute terror. He had no respect for other people or their space. He turned on the lights late at night as he rummaged through stuff in the room. He would pace back and forth as if to occupy his mind or satisfy a nervous tick. He would request snacks in the middle of the night, and then bring them back to the room and munch on them making a noise as if he were chewing into a microphone. Sounds dramatic, but at 2:00 a.m., the sound of someone eating Fritos beside you doesn't exactly foster a peaceful night's sleep. When he used the bathroom, he always seemed to miss the toilet bowl. I would find urine all over the toilet seat and little puddles of it on the floor around the toilet. He would get up to use the bathroom a few times during the night, each time leaving the light on. I would then have to get up and turn off the light. He didn't seem to mind the lights on as he slept with all of the blankets completely covering his head and body.

He stayed only a couple of nights before he got into a fight with another patient over an argument they had. As a result, he was sent to another unit where aggressive patients were treated. While I felt bad he couldn't control his anger, I was relieved to have some personal space again. However, it wasn't long before the bed was filled.

Saturday

I woke up on schedule around 7:00 a.m. It was Saturday, and my first thought was that I'd made it to the weekend. Two more days. Six more meals. Two more nights.

A few weeks before my suicide attempt, I read a book by Victor Frankl called *Man's Search for Meaning*. I read a few books in search for hope and abatement of my intense depression before I decided to try and end it all. That book was among the few I read and among the few that stuck with me. It brought me strength when I had none because if the Jews in the concentration camps could survive such inhumanity, then I, too, could survive the emotional aloneness and abandonment that I felt. But how did they do it? How do people survive through such trauma?

Victor spends the greater part of his book uncovering the secret to finding purpose and meaning in a life that faced such opposition and depression. He stated that those who had family were the ones who had something to look forward to. They endured their tribulation with the hope that they would one day be reunited with those whom they loved. In my deepest moments of desperation sitting under the burning fluorescent lights of the psych ward, I felt what he meant. I understood the assignment. I shared this revelation with my sister as we spoke on the phone. I told her that the one thing that was helping me survive was the thought that I would one day see her again. And I held on to that thought for dear life.

That afternoon, the doctor came over to see me and check in. He spent less than two minutes with me asking about how I was doing. He said that they were preparing for my discharge on Monday. I asked him what time, and he told me that it could be as early as 8:00 a.m. I asked him about paperwork and how that all worked. He told me that they would get my papers in order and signed by Monday morning. I knew from seeing other people discharged that they had to have their paperwork before the day of discharge, so I asked him if the papers could be signed over the weekend. He assured me they could be.

That weekend, a few new admissions arrived at the unit.

That night as I lay in bed, my roommate sparked an unwanted conversation. I rolled my eyes and gave him short answers, hoping he would get the message. He then asked me what my discharge date was. I told him on Monday.

And he said, "Oh, are you sure?"

"Yes, why?"

"I have been here enough to know that when they tell you one thing, they mean another. Have they changed your discharge date before, telling you that you'd leave one day but then change it to the next?" he asked.

I replied to him with a bit of concern in my voice, "They were thinking about discharging me on Wednesday, then changed it to Friday, then changed it to Monday."

He said, "Yeah, see? They do that to try and get you to crack. They would rather have you freak out here than lose it out there. They want to see if you're ready to go. It's a test."

This thought terrified me. Were they testing me? Were they messing with me? Were they going to decline my discharge date on Monday? My anxiety immediately went from a three to a ten.

"This is my third time here, so I know how things work. And this is your first time here, isn't it? Yeah, they mess with you to see how you'll respond. I wouldn't bank on Monday, man," my roommate said.

I didn't say anything further, but I could feel my heart begin to pound heavily inside my chest. I lost my breath, and I feared I would never get out of there.

Sunday

I woke up on Sunday in fear. Would I be discharged on Monday? Later that day as I was reading, I noticed that the director of nursing came to the unit. He motioned me over to speak with him. I slowly rose from my seat and approached him, unsure of what he would have to say to me. I felt butterflies in my stomach, and my hands began to clam up.

He saw me approach. "Hey, Jordan! I heard about your discharge tomorrow."

"Yes, that's the plan. Do you know anything about it?" I asked.

"As far as I know, everything is set, and paperwork has been signed for you. We are encouraged by your family support."

I let out a sigh of relief and said, "Okay, thank you."

He replied, "Take care of yourself, OK? You're a special kid, and you're going to do really great things; I can see it. And if there's anything you need, ever, we're here for you."

I cracked a smile and said, "Thank you. I appreciate it." I walked back to my seat, relieved by his words. I felt like I could start to breathe again. Two more meals, and I would be out of there. I could do it.

That night I lay down on that hard mattress for the last time. I'd made it. I made it to the end. I almost couldn't believe it. While I was so happy, there was still a tiny part of me that thought, *What if they are playing you?* Only time would tell. I closed my eyes and chose to lean toward the thought that on Monday I would walk through those locked doors and reunite with my family. The scene I'd imagined would finally play out.

Monday

The next morning, I was awoken by the tech coming in and saying, "Jordan! Get up. Your family is downstairs waiting to pick you up."

My heart jumped. Had I heard that correctly? My family was here! I jumped out of bed. I packed up the few clothes I had along with my journal and a few other papers. I looked through the arts and crafts I'd done throughout the week and came across the sand art I'd done the first day I was there. I looked at it as if it were stained with the most desolate feelings I'd ever experienced. It was covered with depression and anxiety, feelings of complete aloneness and an indescribable emotional ache that's only known to those who feel it. It felt heavy. It was blemished with my past. And I didn't want any part of it. I folded it and dropped it in the trash can.

I signed a few papers. The tech took my vitals and walked me to the lobby. As I got into the elevator one last time, I thought, *This is it. It's done.* I was happy and nervous. I felt embarrassed to see my family. After all, here I was, Jordan Roberts, walking out of a psych hospital. The disruption and scare I'd caused for my family. The disappointment. The fear. The shame. Was I ready for what was to come?

I had an influx of raw emotions as I felt the elevator slowly moving downward; I watched as we passed through the floors—three, two, one— *ding!* The elevator doors opened, and we proceeded through another set of locked doors into the lobby.

Chapter Thirty One

My dad, mom, and sister were all there sitting in the corner waiting for me. As I walked through the doors, my dad jumped up and literally ran over to hug me. We embraced in a long hug that gave way to tears. I felt like I was finally safe. I then hugged my sister, who gave me an affirming squeeze as I saw my mom. It was almost as if she offered a reluctant hug, which I held on to longer than she did. My mom never showed a lot of emotion, so I know that this was difficult for her. I can't even begin to describe what I'd put her through. And I'm afraid I will never know. The weight of being in the psych ward was lifted off me. When I heard the big, metal door shut, I knew that I was done with that place.

The four of us walked out to my parents' white Chevy Equinox. I got in the back seat, my sister sat next to me, and my parents rode in the front. My dad started up the vehicle, and we went to the hotel where they'd stayed the night so that I could finally shower and get cleaned up. I'd showered once in seven days and hadn't shaved at all. My face itched, and I looked like I'd given up on myself, which I guess I had. I couldn't wait to shave.

When we arrived at the hotel, my dad handed me a plastic ziplock bag with my phone and charger in it. I looked at it for a few seconds, deciding whether or not to turn it on, then put it down without opening it. Instead, I immediately pulled out some new clothes from a suitcase that had been packed for me and took a long, hot shower. It felt so good to have the water run over my body without the fear of someone watching or coming into the bathroom. I felt relieved standing under the hot stream pulsing from the showerhead against my weak, tired body. My family had packed my loofa and my favorite shower gel. I lathered up and felt like I washed away the stank of that horrible hospital. It hurt when I shaved that morning. Shaving those long hairs with a razor wasn't ideal, but I felt like a new man getting clean and shaven.

When I was dressed and ready to go, I walked down to the lobby and sat on one of the couches while I waited for my parents and sister to pack their things and load up the car. As I sat in the lobby, I dug my phone out and decided to turn it on. I wondered what was waiting for me as I hadn't had it in over a week (including my time in the ED). I had several missed phone calls, texts messages, and even some Facebook posts asking where I was and if anyone had heard from me. It was nice to know people cared.

One of the first people I texted was Mattie. I told her I was sorry about going MIA and explained to her what had happened. She reached out with such compassion and love. We normally texted every day, so not hearing from me was out of character, which had made her worried.

I texted with a few other close friends and then called Andrea from the neuro ICU where I worked. I valued (and still value) her friendship. I wanted to keep her updated with what was going on. She, too, received the news with such grace and empathy. Her concern wasn't work-related, but that I was truly OK. Work came second with her, and I appreciated it.

Before we left, my sister, Mom, Dad, and I met in the lobby for a continental breakfast. As I was sitting there picking at my bagel with cream cheese, I looked around and thought the last time I was in a hotel like this was when I was a flight attendant. I gave a little smile and looked back down at my bagel.

The car ride to my sister's house was about ten hours, most of which was spent in silence. I don't think any of us really knew how to act or react to what had happened. I know I didn't. I felt awkward, and I was eager to investigate the cause of such a monumental disruption to my life and the lives of those around me. But one of my sister's greatest qualities is not judging people for the pain they endure in life. She loves with open arms, never giving a second thought.

During my week in the hospital, I lost twelve pounds. I had no interest in eating, and the food was less than palatable. I made myself drink water so that I could continue to flush out the drugs from my system, but that was it.

It was around eight in the evening when we arrived at my sister's house. My parents came in for a few minutes, used the bathroom, and filled up on coffee before they continued their journey home, which was an additional four hours. I'd assumed they would spend the night, but they had to return home. I felt bad for their long journey. And I felt like it was my fault, which it was. Everything felt very robotic and monotonous. The air had a numbing feeling, but no one dared bring it up. Even at the critical time, thoughts and emotions were kept at bay. And all I could think about was how I would adapt to my new life in the sterile bubble.

Chapter Thirty Two

My sister told me that I would be staying in the spare room in the basement. I'd been to her house many times before, so I was familiar with the layout. When my parents left, I went down to my new room, where I found my bed set up with my sheets and pillows. I also noticed two teddy bears that had been gifted to me several years prior purposefully placed on the bed. My bookshelf was set up with some of the books I owned along with my essential oils and a few candles.

I saw my belongings, but it wasn't my place. I was taken aback because I wasn't ready to see all of my things there. For some reason, I'd thought that everything would be in storage. I walked around the room noticing all of my possessions, but feeling lost. I opened the drawers to the dresser and found my clothes neatly folded. I sifted through a few documents lying on the dresser being transported back to my life in Chicago. I sat on the floor and stared at the carpet in a daze. A few minutes later, my sister came in to see if there was anything I needed. I told her no.

She asked if the room was OK, and I said, "Yes, a little weird seeing all of my stuff here." She told me that she could understand it would be an adjustment. I nodded and said good night.

I slept in late the next day, though periodically waking up to the sound of my four-year-old nephew running around on the hardwood floors upstairs. It was nice to be back in my own bed, but I felt like I was in an unfamiliar place. It was my sister's house, yet I was sleeping in my bed. It didn't feel right. I didn't know what to do, so I stayed lying there tossing from one side to the other. Eventually, I rolled out of bed, climbed the stairs and navigated my way to the kitchen, where I was greeted by my sister and nephew. I indulged myself in a cup of coffee, something I had been deprived of in the psych unit.

I sat at the kitchen table while sipping on my coffee and feeling the nudges from my nephew to play with him, but all I wanted to do was crawl back into bed. I couldn't settle in my mind what had happened. It was like I had been teleported through two different worlds into two different lives.

One day I was living my life in Chicago, working full time, going out to bars, living my gay life, and relaxing in my one-bedroom apartment on Sheridan Road. The next thing I knew, I'd woken up in a psych ward relying on a hazy memory of how I'd got there. Then I found myself living with my sister in West Virginia, surrounded by noises of children on a daily basis. The shock took hold of me.

I tried to piece together the traumatic events that had just taken place while getting my bearings in this new environment I'd found myself in. I felt as if I'd been dropped off in a foreign land, which doesn't even make sense because I knew exactly where I was. But I was completely stunned. I experienced a mental and emotional paralysis that rendered me near lifeless.

I felt like I had to immediately fill a role of uncle, brother, and helper when my whole reality felt like an uncontrollable whirlwind. One would think that all of these tasks would provide a wonderful distraction from the current stressors, but my mind felt broken; my emotions were wounded and there wasn't a balm strong enough to heal me.

My sister and my parents discussed with me about getting into biblical counseling. I let out a sigh and thought, "Not this again." They had researched counselors from a biblical agency and showed me a list on the internet of men they thought could help me. I reluctantly read their bios and felt no connection with any of them. I said that I didn't feel like these people could help me because what I needed was professional help from individuals who specialize in LGBTQ+ people and those who struggle with suicide. But the rebuttal was always the same—the answer is in the Bible. I didn't have the strength to defend myself, so I agreed to go with one of the counselors. I scrolled through application, which was extensive and detailed. The first question read, "*Explain your relationship with the Lord and your salvation story."* At point I closed the computer and voiced that I wouldn't do it. I got up from the table and went downstairs to my room.

A few days later, I told my sister that I was going to look for my own therapist and heal in the way that I felt was the best way. I didn't want people throwing Bible verses at me or creating a space that was disapproving of me. I needed a safe space of acceptance and love. And I needed someone to help me get to the root of the problem and what caused such a downward spiral. I searched online and found a woman who specialized in the areas I was looking for. I contacted her and we set up an appointment.

I wanted to spend time alone, but I also didn't want to be disrespectful of my family. I felt that if I spent too much time in my room, they would either think something was wrong or that I didn't want to spend time with them. But my sister was very gracious and understood my needing to heal.

Every morning, I woke up with my heart feeling heavy inside my chest. I didn't have the strength to be human. I didn't have the strength to interact. A few days turned into three weeks, and I felt myself slipping away again. My mind and emotions felt fragile. I couldn't get a handle on what had happened to me. My sister constantly asked me what I needed and how she could best help me, and I always replied with an "I don't know." It wasn't a lie because I really didn't know what I needed. I didn't know how to help myself. I'd never tried to recover from suicide before. To say the least, I felt numb.

To help get me through the first several weeks, I watched a lot of *RuPaul's Drag Race* and reconnected with friends. One person who played a vital role during this time was my dear friend Mattie. Her presence and words encouraged me more than ever during this unprecedented time. She let me talk about my feelings, let me be open and real with how I was feeling, and gave me insightful feedback about how to continue forward in a positive way. She was my rock, always there when I needed her. I remember telling her on a daily basis that I wanted to go home. I just couldn't get over the reality that I no longer lived in Chicago. That my stuff was now in my sister's house. And I was now living in West Virginia. I didn't have a car. I didn't have a job.

For the first three weeks, I didn't go anywhere besides run errands with my sister. I was living by someone else's rules, on someone else's timeline, under someone else's roof. I remember pacing my bedroom floor and screaming into pillows, praying I would find a way to improve my life.

Mattie always knew what to say to assuage my turbulent emotions. She's the kind of friend who responds with sound advice and a level-headed perspective. She is intelligent but humble, honest but gentle. The welcoming aura she created made it feel like home when around her. She was a friend and a mighty confidant.

A few days after I'd settled in at my sister's, Ariel, my childhood friend, came to visit me. Reconnecting with her filled my soul. Her presence was calming as she spoke with encouraging words. Perhaps the most therapeutic part of her visit was the fact that she was physically present. And that tangible interaction is what I needed in those desperate moments.

One December afternoon, my sister's family and I decorated the Christmas tree in the living room. As we strategically placed the lights and colorful bulbs on the tree, my sister asked me again how I was doing and what she could do to help. We discussed that I was struggling but that I was hopeful because I knew that this wasn't my end. Rather, her house served as a healing space—a place I could be while I got back on my feet.

Chapter Thirty Three

*A*major stressor for me was the coexisting that had to take place—an openly gay man now living with family who didn't share the same fundamental values. I'd returned to the traumatic place I'd worked so hard to get out of. But the very issue that made want to flee from the beginning was the very culprit that forced me back. Trauma was compounding on trauma, and I felt like I still couldn't breathe. I had to heal in an environment that—while loving—was unaccepting of me.

It is important to note that I have never once felt unloved by my family. I have been incredibly blessed to have been surrounded with a lot of love and support throughout my entire life. There was one area that lacked support—my sexual identity, which turned out to be the most important.

When I came out to my family, there was love. And I'm grateful for that because there are a lot of people who didn't have love and (sometimes) faced violence. And my heart goes out to them. But what my family couldn't do for me was accept me. Not being accepted felt like not being chosen.

However, I do remember one phone call I received from my oldest brother (yes, the one who used to call me fairy and antagonize my gayness) and his wife while I was in the psych unit. On that call, they both told me that they loved and accepted me for who I am, no matter what. It was in that moment that I finally heard what I'd been wanting to hear and felt what I needed to feel. Then I understood the difference between love and acceptance. Love is the willingness to acknowledge but not participate; love and acceptance is acknowledging and participating with genuine motives.

When your family says that they can't accept an integral part of you, it is like saying they can't accept you. Family is supposed to be the people you trust the most and the place where you feel the safest. Losing that is the loneliest feeling in the world. And that was a catalyst that sprung me into the darkest depths of misery.

This idea of finding both love and acceptance is so important because it serves as the foundation for my mental health demise.

I was never able to be real with my family. Every time we were together, I had to put on a mask and play a performance. It was an exhausting charade. I couldn't share my thoughts and feelings, so I had to hide. No one truly ever knew who I was. I was always told to smile more, talk more, participate more, act happier, and so on. But how was I supposed to do those things when I couldn't be myself? I wanted to express myself, but I couldn't because I didn't want to make myself or anyone else uncomfortable.

I will not, however, pass blame to anyone for anything surrounding this topic. People have a right to believe in what they want. My family's beliefs happen to go against my beliefs, which has caused tremendous hurt, and that's OK. We'll always be bonded with love, and it'll remain steadfast. Just as I've gone through a hard time, I know that my family has carried their own burdens with the events that led up to this story. And the fact that I hurt them hurts me.

It's important to see the gap that's left when one is loved but not accepted the way they are. And it's paramount to have a conversation about these topics. Over time, I've been able to discuss with members of my family the struggles that come with being gay. And while our beliefs didn't change, the door to conversation was opened.

During that time, I was supposed to be healing, but I wasn't. My voice was silenced by the echoes of the worldview that was set before me. I'm glad I was raised with a moral compass and that I was taught the difference between right and wrong. I'm grateful I had such a loving upbringing that built within me a strong sense of ethics and positive decision making. But the thing I mourn the most is this idea of religion that was woven within my background, one that was one of exclusivity instead of inclusivity. This faith silenced me. There was always a voice in the back of my head that told me that I was wrong, and perhaps, that was the reason I struggled to move forward. I cannot explain the daily ethical battle I have with myself and how it wears down on me. I'm consumed by the question, *What if I'm wrong?*

One afternoon, the story of Rahab came to my mind. So I looked online for a Bible to read this story. Rahab was a prostitute who risked her life to hide two people who were used by God to defeat the pagan city of Jericho. When asked about the two men, Rahab said that she knew nothing of them. In return, Rahab was instructed to put out a red cloth from a window so she and her family would be spared from dying when the city of Jericho was invaded. Despite all of this feeling a bit odd, Rahab did what she was asked, and she was spared. In fact, she became part of Jesus's lineage.

I thought about Rahab. If she, a prostitute, can be used of God, then why can't I? When learning about my decision to accept being gay, many people in my biblical circles attributed my lifestyle to one of unholiness, to which they would frequently say, "You have strayed from the Lord." It's not like I felt like I was a prostitute, but those words cut deep because I no longer felt like I was a good person. I felt judged because I decided to embrace who I was inside. And because of that, I felt like God couldn't use me or that I couldn't be a Christian because, according to my upbringing, I was living outside of God's will and plan for my life.

However, Rahab encouraged me. She demonstrated faith, and it saved her. Why can't I do the same thing? What God wants is for me to come to Him with a willing heart to know Him. He wants a relationship. I don't have to present a mile-long list of rules I kept in order to find favor in His eyes. He wants just me, as I am. Just like Rahab.

And the different conversations I had with the gay pastor I went on a date with in Chicago, my brother-in-law, and Mr. Jones came back to my mind. I understood that I may not have the answers to all of the questions. I may not know why there's so much bad in the world. But with all the bad, there's also a lot of good. And we use the good to outweigh the bad. The key to knowing God and strengthening my faith is accepting the fact that sometimes we don't have the answers. But being willing to use the good we've been given to improve the world around us is what we need.

Also, Mr. Jones's words came back to me as he said that God deals with us individually. It's not a competition. My life won't be measured against someone else's standard. It's just God and me.

The Gospel is simple: Jesus gave His life for me because He loves me. He showed His power over my shortcomings by defeating death so that I can have life. I can either accept to believe that or think it is just a history lesson. I chose to believe it because throughout the course of my life there is one thing that I cannot deny—God's presence in my life. He's always been faithful to me, and now it was my turn to be faithful to Him. I took off my glasses of legalistic Baptist Christianity, and I replaced them with vision of love.

I finally understood that God wants me. And there's no catch. My view of Christianity and religion was tainted by a level of holiness that was impossible to achieve. I had to display my holiness to show that I was a Christian, and if I wasn't completely focused on being holier today than I was yesterday, then there was a problem with my spirituality. My focus centered around this idea of holiness instead of a relationship with Jesus. But I realized that holiness doesn't define my relationship. God doesn't want my vain works. He just wants me. I can let go of those legalistic practices that poisoned my view of who God really is and solely trust in the person God says He is.

God used my suicide attempt to reveal Himself to me. He restored me from my hopelessness and rescued me from death. I know that there is purpose left for me. And I want to share this story as a testament that, even though our struggle is real, there is still hope. And God is always willing to meet us in our personal hell to carry us home. I asked where God was when I needed Him most. And I found that He was always there.

He was with me as I dealt with the cruelty of my bullies.

His kindness was revealed when he gave me the power of music.

He walked with me through countries and experiences.

He remained in the background when I indulged my physical desires.

He restored me from my abusers.

He carried my soul when I let go.

He was in the hymns I sang for comfort.

He was in the glimpse of hope that came when needed most.

He came in the form of faith that remained constant.

He was in the truth that brought me home.

I want this story to be a source of hope to those who are struggling the way that I was. You don't have to be religious to find hope, faith, or love. It's already in you. You were created perfectly the way you are to fulfill a specific purpose. Sometimes the road is hard, but we have to keep moving forward and the plan will be revealed for us. My gay pride is based in the peace I find knowing that I'm loved by God and others. When I understood that, I was able to be kind to myself and give myself the life I deserve. And I know you can do the same.

Throughout my writing, I'd asked myself the question, *Why me?* Why did I have to struggle like I did in my life? But then I stopped asking myself, *Why me?* and asked, *Why not me?* I'm stronger than my greatest battle. And I believe we already have inside of us the power to conquer our demons. Instead of looking at my struggles with negativity, I chose to view them in a positive way because they can be used for good. I can have a voice, and I'm resolved to speak my truth loud and clear. Maya Angelou said, "There is no greater agony than bearing an untold story inside you." For too long, I hid my story; I hid myself. But no longer will I put myself through that kind of mistreatment. And I will tell my story of trauma and redemption because we all need hope.

Chapter Thirty Four

How did I get out of the muck I was in? First, I was put on a medication regime that worked for me. By the way, there's no shame in taking medication to improve your mental health and stability. It's important to discuss these options because they could be a life saver.

Second, I removed myself from the environment that I was in. I removed the toxicity, and that helped me to heal properly. I stopped trying to find fulfillment in superfluous things like alcohol and sex. I stopped seeking men out for validation. And I still haven't gone to the gym. And I didn't need to in order to find contentment with who I am. Instead, I focused on what my future looked like.

After I'd settled into my sister's house, I had a phone call with my nurse manager about next steps. They were attentive to my needs and helped in any way that they could. We decided a one-month leave of absence was in my best interest and then determine if I needed more time after that. But after a few weeks, I could tell that I wouldn't last more than a month without working or having anything to do professionally. I needed something to occupy my mind and my time. Unfortunately, I knew that moving back to Chicago during my recovery wasn't a good option.

So, I opened up my computer one evening and began researching temporary nurse jobs in the area as well as in Virginia near my parents. I found a couple of options and sent out inquiries. A few days later, I received a phone call from a nice woman who answered my questions and walked me through the steps of possibly applying to these jobs I'd found. She also mentioned the idea of working at a place called the University of Virginia Medical Center (UVA) in Charlottesville, Virginia. I'd never heard of it, but it sounded like a good place. It was four hours from my sister's and two hours from my parents' house. I thought about moving, but I was nervous my family would think it was too soon.

I fought the urge to please others and took control of the direction I wanted my life to go in instead. I knew I had to make a change for myself and that change included getting a job. I called my nurse manager and told him that I didn't see a way for me to come back to Chicago within the next six months. I wanted to be honest because fostering that relationship was important to me. Being honest is always the best option because people want what's best for you. So that day, I sent my manager a letter of resignation, which was accepted. And I was told that if I'd ever want to come back in the future to give them a call.

I told my parents and my sister that I'd resigned from my position in Chicago and was looking for other opportunities closer to where they lived. They were supportive of my decision to start working again, but strongly encouraged me to put my mental health first, which I did. The prospect of a new job excited me and the fact that I had support from my family gave me more momentum to find a job.

I called the lady who I'd been talking to about UVA and told her that I'd like to move forward with the job. That same afternoon, I received an offer to work on the COVID unit at the university hospital. I gladly accepted and prepared to move to Charlottesville. Again, I planned to move to a place I'd never been to before.

Here's the third way I improved myself— removing myself from a toxic environment; doing this allowed me to rediscover who I was and my purpose. The power I discovered within myself silenced the communal voices that told me I had no value. The pressure to be to impress the world around me weakened as I redirected my focus onto myself instead of onto others. And I did that by giving myself space to breathe.

Working at UVA was supposed to be a temporary job to provide some income and a way to gradually ease myself back into the workforce. Because of the temporary nature, I looked on Airbnb for a place to live for three months. I found a beautiful, quaint cottage set in the woods of a place called Palmyra, about forty minutes from UVA. I did not love the idea of a long commute, but there was something serene and comforting that drew me to this place. I contacted the owner, and after some messaging, I decided to rent this idyllic little house in the woods.

The cottage was a beautiful one-bedroom, arcadian abode. Driving through the winding roads deep into the country made me question my decisions because I'd never thought I'd find myself choosing to live in the country again, but I kept driving until I arrived at what would become my haven. When I walked through the door of this rustic chalet, I was greeted with warmth and a smell of lavender and mint. I looked around at the perfectly tidy interior and thought, *I'm going to be just fine.*

The cottage was on the same property of the owner's house, who were, by the way, wonderful people. They invited me over on several occasions to share dinner and play Sequence. Hospitality was their gift, and I thoroughly enjoyed sharing that short time with them. It reminded me of my time in Peru when I'd gather with friends to share a meal, play board games, or watch movies. It was about relationship building—something I'd missed.

The forty-minute drive to and from work was not ideal, but living in that bucolic nook provided me a wonderful disconnect from work that I know was important for my wellbeing during that time. Living in my new quiet, serene oasis gave me newness of life as I focused on myself because I did not have the distractions I'd once had to get me off course. I was finally in a place where I could focus on my purpose and be truly happy.

Rediscovering my purpose was crucial during this phase of my life. When I made others' thoughts about me more important than what I thought about myself, I lost sight of who I was. I no longer enjoyed the things I used to enjoy because I wanted what someone else had. I was adding up my own tallies with someone else's rule book, and that doesn't work.

When I stopped comparing myself to others, I slowly began to find my purpose. And part of my purpose in this world is to help people, especially through my job. I no longer go into work wishing I was someone else; rather, I find enjoyment in the fact that I have a unique experience every day to help someone in a new way. I remain focused on doing my task well which keeps me anchored and the rest will work itself out.

Fourth, I found a bedside nursing job that allowed me to prioritize my mental health. Working at UVA was more than I could have ever asked for. It was the perfect introduction back to work after going through the mental health crisis I'd been through. The first day of work I was greeted with many smiling faces and people who were eager to make me feel welcome and supported.

The manager, Ryan, came up to me, shook my hand and welcomed me to the unit with a big smile on his face. From that moment, I could tell there was something special about him. He was a manager that believed in his people, and he worked tirelessly to create an environment that supported the staff. The atmosphere that he created was free of stress. I actually enjoyed going into work. On many occasions I'd think to myself, *did I really find a stress-free nursing job?* And I'd certainly did. My coworkers and managers have now become lifelong friends.

In the beginning, they did not know who I was or what I was going through, but they accepted me with open arms and helped me in ways they'll never know. One of the most impactful things that I noticed was that they allowed me to be me without question.

I was only supposed to be at UVA for three months; however, those three months turned into almost two years. And within those two years, I was able to debut my role as a preceptor (teacher) to new nurses, not once, but three times and get involved with some leadership roles. What I gained from UVA are treasures that I will carry with me throughout the rest of my days.

I wanted to include this portion in this text as a testament that things always tend to work themselves out. I know that it sounds cliché, but the light has to come after things are really dark. Whatever you're going through in life, please know that things will get better. They always do. The worst action you can take is to stop trying. Never stop fighting, because, one day, you will win. Always fight for one more day; the victory could be tomorrow.

Fifth, I accepted myself for who God made me to be. I determined that loving myself unconditionally trumped defeating myself with the legalist, Christian practices I was force-fed during my developmental and college years. I was living by man's standard instead of God's, which planted lies about who I was and allowed years of bitterness to undermine my well-being.

Finally, I chose to trust in God again as the source of my hope, progress, blessings and healing. And I was able to do that because I came to understand who God was. In the beginning chapter, I asked if I had ever felt connected to God, and I really hadn't until I came to an understanding that God sees beyond my failures. He's not the God who I couldn't please with my empty praise and endless works, but the true God of love who wants me for who I am; I'm made with purpose and without error.

Backspace means to delete or remove a character in order to start over. I had to take a step back and remove the erroneous thinking that I couldn't please God if I chose to be gay. I had to reset and realize that God had always loved me, even though I was told being gay was a sin. Sometimes we have to undo what we'd learned in our childhood because as we evolve, we grow. What we are taught isn't always right; when we find our truth, we will be set free. Sometimes we have to start over by erasing old habits, which is tough. But what we gain is much more than what we had.

No matter what you're going through, I want you to know that you're not alone. I don't know what your struggle is, but I want you to know that you're exactly who you were created to be; and you're exactly where you're supposed to be. Choose to keep walking forward. And if you feel like you've come to the end of your rope, seeing no way out, know that there's more beyond what you can see.

If you have tried everything in your search for fulfillment but have been left with dissatisfaction like I was, know there is still hope beyond what seems impossible. I know that life can be a burden, and that burden can feel too heavy to carry at times, but you're stronger, better, and more courageous than you think you are. If faith, religion, or God isn't your thing, know that I'm standing with you.

If you're a person of faith, but you feel as if faith as failed you in some way, give it another try. Even if you've trusted God once before but felt nothing in return, like I did, don't give up. Maybe the god who failed you isn't the true God that I have come to know. Our bad days aren't foreign to the Omniscient One; rather, they are opportunities to see Him. Trust that you'll always be rescued.

It is through our victories and failures that we learn who we are. I believe I am better off now than I was when I first started. I am better off because I failed miserably. My experiences shaped my decisions and influenced my thoughts. My worldview served as a catalyst to bring me through the tortures of my sexual journey. I never imagined I would go through the things I went through, but in a serious way, I would not change anything. After all, I wouldn't be writing this had the following events not happened the way that they did. Through it all, God's grace brought me above the limitations I put on myself, and saved me from the pit I dug. My experiences were tools that built a better structure that I call my life, my morals, my boundaries and my thinking.

I struggled with faith for a long time because so much responsibility was tied to it. Faith held the key to where I'd would spend eternity, and it was hard to grasp that. I didn't want to mess it up on a technicality. It took me many years to realize that faith didn't have to be difficult. I didn't need some miraculous story to have enough faith to be saved. Faith is believing God is who He says He is. Period.

The faith that I have is the same faith the thief on the cross had when he pleaded to Jesus to save his soul; it's the same faith Rahab had when she placed the scarlet thread outside of her window. I thought that because I was gay, I wouldn't be able to have enough faith to make it to heaven. But I was wrong. All you have to do is believe. And that's when my new genesis began.

Yours is waiting for you.

Chapter Thirty Five

I have one more thought that I'd like to share regarding gender roles.

The idea of gender roles and more specifically biblical masculinity was a pillar in the worldview that was taught to me through my formative years. And there were two views of this. First, the secular world had a standard of what masculinity entailed. And this included being a leader, making a lot of money, having a strong mind and body, leaving your underwear on the floor, and eating wings and drinking beer while checking out women at Hooter's.

Men should not cry, but be rough and rugged; however, they should also be sensitive to understand women and show empathy. But they can't be too sensitive lest they appear weak and vulnerable. Masculinity means having control and expected to know the answers to everything, but not being arrogant. To be a real man means not having the appearance of doing something even remotely feminine.

In addition to all of that (perhaps with the exception of going to Hooter's), the second view is the role of biblical masculinity. Biblical masculinity placed men over women as the leader of the family. The biblical man provides for his family; he is the figure head that binds the familial unit together. The hierarchy goes men, women, then children.

The church did an excellent job at separating men and women with women's luncheons and men's Bible studies and prayer groups. There'd often be men's weekend camping trips where the male congregants would gather together, talk about their battles and learn how to improve their masculinity while they cooked freshly caught fish over an open flame.

The ladies would stay home and engage in their own activities. I was often invited and expected to attend these men's outings, but I didn't like or understand why it had to be segregated. I didn't feel comfortable around a lot of men because I was incidentally taught that I wasn't masculine by the echoes that told me I'd never measure up. The masculine figure that was portrayed, both biblical and secular, was not the type of man I was inside, so I struggled to find common ground with them. And I felt like an outsider.

When I was sixteen years old, my parents bought me a used Honda Civic because that was the car that fit their budget within a drivable distance; I loved that they gave me a car for my birthday; it was a special day. But it was purple. To my parents, it was just a color, and they didn't think anything of it. I, however, felt embarrassed because I was afraid that people would make fun of me for having a purple car being that purple isn't typically known for being a man's color.

So when I drove to school the next day, I didn't tell anyone about my new car, and I parked in the farthest parking spot I could find. It wasn't long, though, before my friends found out about my new wheels, and they congratulated me because getting a car was a huge deal, especially for a teenager. And everyone wanted a ride in it.

I was delighted everyone was supportive, and I got over the embarrassment of driving around the purple vehicle. But it was this idea of gender roles that made me self-conscious of the color of my new automobile. And this embarrassment fed my anxiety, which robbed me of truly enjoying the receiving process. This erroneous pattern of thinking resided in my mind, influencing me to go against my natural inclination for the sake of honoring the system that placed men and women in separate boxes.

I did not know where I fit. I was biologically a man, but I didn't feel like a man. I couldn't fulfill my duty and role as a man that was set for me by a societal and biblical standard. What do you do when you feel like you don't belong in the space that was determined for you? You want to be somewhere in the middle, but that's not an option. You want to discuss these feelings with someone, but the fear of rejection or the fact that that you won't be understood is so great that you keep it all to yourself. The world looks at you funny because they don't know what to do with what's different. The world is obsessed with normalcy and rejects anything that challenges the system.

I always thought it interesting that if a woman wore men's clothing, no one cared, but if a man wore women's clothing, then an uproar broke out. And I saw a lot of women in men's clothing, especially shorts and shirts in the name of modesty. In my biblical circle, it was modest for women to wear shorts below the knee and not leave the shoulders uncovered. Today, if I see a woman in board shorts, I think lesbian. But to a conservative Christian it's modesty and will be praised.

It's okay for a woman not to wear make-up, wear baggy clothing and give off a masculine appearance, but if a man were to put on eyeliner and mid-thigh shorts, parents would cover their kids' eyes and walk on the other side of the street as if this man was somehow rebellious and sinning. Since when was putting on mascara a sin according to the Bible?

Putting on make-up or wearing high heels is nothing more than feeling beautiful and empowered. It is no different than going to the gym to work on that killer body and flexing in the mirror. It's a vehicle for self-love and inspiration. But my mode of feeling powerful is demonized because it goes against a man-made tradition.

Being in the middle of gender identity fed the parasite of inadequacy. I was forced to put on a mask because people didn't want to see the real me. And let's be honest, I was scared to be real with the world because I was indirectly taught that being me was unacceptable. No one wants to be insupportable, so we do the natural thing and work tirelessly to be exactly who we aren't. Running in the opposite direction messes with your mind until it becomes so warped that mental health trauma takes up residence and eats at your soul one thought at a time. Even medication has its limits. And it's only a matter of time before exhaustion gives way to defeat.

The cycle stops when we stop believing in what people tell us to believe and discover truth for ourselves. Not fitting into the gender role box that I was born into will always be a point of stress for me, but I no longer allow it to control my behavior or my decisions. As a society, we are slowly moving in the direction of acceptance and inclusion for all people. It's not perfect, but it's better. And there are many more resources available for those who feel like they don't fit where they were told to fit. The door to this conversation is much easier to open now that it was ten years ago. So we must keep building the force for advocacy and inclusion in how we deal with people in the LGBTQ+ community.

So what's the point of this? Feeling like you don't' fit where you're supposed to is a miserable feeling. It's even worse because it can feel like no one can or will ever understand you. The point of these words is to remind you that you are not alone. Every part of you is intentional and useful. You can't control who you were born to be, but you can control how you use your beautiful parts (that some have labeled as ugly) to improve the world around you. You are who you are on purpose, so use your uniqueness with intention and power. The passion you have is rare. Stop hiding and tell your story.

Afterword

How to Come Out to Family, Spouse, or Friends

I wanted to include a portion of this book dedicated to coming out to family, friends, or both. Deciding to come out is a huge milestone and should only be done when one feels ready to do so. Sadly, some people don't have the option to choose when they come out because they're outed by their peers. To these people, I'm deeply sorry, but there's also something in here for you, too.

I'm in no way an expert on these issues and the advice I give is solely based off of how my experience was. I want to share my personal thoughts with the hope that they can be useful to you and your coming out story.

Determine when You're Ready

Coming out is your story and should be done under your timeline. So how do you know when you're ready? It took several years of battling before I decided it was time for me to stop suppressing the person I was inside. The world, your friends, and family deserve to know you. But it's hard to reveal such a vulnerable part of yourself, especially when you grow up the way I did. There's a weight of shame that comes with accepting yourself as gay because all you've been taught your whole life is that being a homosexual is one of the worst of sins and God hates it. Yikes. Who would want to admit to that then?

As discussed in the story, I came to the realization that I couldn't change who I was when I'd tried everything else except being myself.

When living how I was supposed to live didn't produce any fruitful out-comes, I opted to allow myself to live openly gay.

When I came out, a few of my friends and other people I knew in college also came out to me privately. I was surprised by how many people shared in the struggle I had. But none of us dared bring it up in Bible college, lest we be very judged. And no one would want to be associated with that kind of sin. There was one exception.

Even with a chance of rejection, one of my best friends in college took the gamble to open up to me about some of his struggles. He told me one night that he was struggling with homosexuality. The news came as a complete shock to me. I had no idea this was where the conversation was going to go, and I certainly wasn't ready to have it. Later, he said that he told me because he was hoping that I, too, would have opened up to him. While he was right about his suspicions of me, I denied being gay. Rather, I drove a knife into his back as I proceeded to tell him that his being gay didn't have to define him; Jesus was stronger than this sin, and we could find him the help he needed to no longer have these unnatural thoughts.

I cringe as I type those words I'd said to him. But in those moments, I wasn't ready to be real with myself and with him. I thought that by confessing to him what he confessed to me would somehow make me less of a Christian, and I wanted to hold the power. I was a hypocrite. And I failed my friend that day. I've since apologized, and we're great friends to this day, though I regret not sharing with him on that night because I just imagine how much better it would have been to bear this burden with someone trustworthy rather than carry it alone.

As evangelicals, we're experts at hiding our struggles because we've somehow equated sin with weakness. And no one wants to appear weak or like they don't have it all together. But if we were honest with ourselves and others, then we could build a community where struggling is equated with growing. It's as if the church has forgotten that we're all human. No one is perfect, but we're obsessed with putting on a show like we're the best thing that's ever happened. We must do better.

I don't know what coming out looks like for you, but we're waiting for whenever you're ready. Fear of coming out is natural. Being vulnerable

Jordan Roberts

is scary. But never forget that you'll always have a community ready to accept you for exactly the person you are. It may take some time to find your community, but people are there. And you're never alone.

A big part of knowing when you're ready to come out is when you're ready to accept yourself. And if you're like me, accepting yourself was very hard to do because every warning bell and siren from Sunday school went off in my head telling me to run away from the sin. But I learned to silence the lies and pick through the weeds until I found what I was looking for. A lot of that came when I understood that God wasn't mad at me; He looked at me the same. I was no surprise for Him.

Accepting myself didn't happen overnight. It took many years to get to that point, and many more even after I came out to continue learning about what it meant to be my authentic self. I still get messages from people in my past who challenge me on my decisions. And I welcome their thoughts because it presents an opportunity for us to dialogue. I learn the most from people who disagree with me, so I enjoy having conversations about these topics.

Accepting what's inside means that you're creating space to grow into your amazing self. Acceptance opens the door to liberation. It won't be without some battle, but the victory is yours.

Understand Who You're Coming Out to and Decide Who to Tell First.

Telling the first person about your sexuality is both frightening and liberating. And most likely, the first person you tell will be someone with whom you have a close relationship, whether that be a family member or friend. The first person I told about my sexuality was my mentor at the college I went to in South America. When I confessed to him, he acted like I'd just admitted I had some sort of communicable disease. And his first thoughts and actions were to "rid" me of this raging sickness. In hindsight, that wasn't the best person or the best environment to reveal my deepest, darkest secrets, but I thought I was doing the right thing at the time.

On the other hand, years later, when I came out to my friend Ariel, she replied with a simple, "I know. I was just waiting for you to tell me."

We both shared a laugh and continued our friendship like nothing had changed. The only thing that did change was the fact that I didn't have to hide anymore.

What I wouldn't advise is coming out on social media before you tell the people closest to you, like the mistake I made with my sister. Even though we're evolving into a tech-savvy society, correspondence through social media is still considered impersonal.

What I failed to realize is that I still hadn't come out to some of my immediate family members and some of my close friends from my Bible college days. I hadn't come out to my sister or my middle brother and his wife. Additionally, I hadn't come out to some of the most influential people in my life during college.

You may be wondering how two years had gone by without revealing to my friends and family that I was gay. But I was so busy focusing on myself and moving forward that I didn't take the time to go back and tell these people about my experiences. I also kept a low profile on Facebook because I had a conservative friends list. Instagram, however, was a different story.

I also didn't tell these individuals because I didn't find the right time, nor did I feel ready to continue to have the same battle over and over again. It was easier to avoid it.

As you can imagine this post came as a shock to them. The person I regret not telling in person the most was my sister. During the summer of that same year, my family and I'd gathered at my sister's house. When I was there, my sister brought up my announcement and asked why I hadn't told her. Taken aback, I didn't quite know how to answer besides saying that it had escaped my mind. You'll remember that years back, I had a conversation with my brother-in-law about my choices, and he kept my trust by keeping that between us. But that night, I was confronted and left to defend my actions to my sister, brother-in-law, mom, and dad. This wasn't a familial conversation; rather, I felt like I was on the stand debating for my life. None of our minds would be changed, so we kept going in circles until one of us eventually agreed to disagree.

Having that conversation was so difficult because I hated disappointing my parents and my family. I hated not being the model child, one they could be proud of. It was very uncomfortable knowing that there was disapproval. But I had to go there. We had to have that conversation.

The thing that stuck out the most during that late-night debate was something my sister said. She said that if they're wrong about the Bible and what it says, then they lose nothing. But if they're right about what the Bible says, then I have everything to lose. She meant that if she was wrong about God's stance on homosexuality, then there was nothing to fear after death; however, if she was right about what God says about homosexuality, then I do have reason to fear death, meaning that I will be separated from God for eternity.

But growing up as a Baptist, I knew exactly what she meant from the beginning. I'm happy to report that since 2018, we've all come a long way. Our debates really have turned into conversations about that which we still don't see eye-to-eye on. But there is still work to be done.

I don't know what your situation looks like, but think through who you want to tell and who deserves to know about you before posting it all over social media. It will save some hard feelings later on.

Be Prepared for Whatever Comes Your Way— Not Everyone Will React the Same

When you've chosen who you're going to tell about your sexuality, I'd assume that you already have a good idea of how they will react. For some people, it'll be a good reaction, but for others, their coming out revelation may not be followed by a celebration and fanfare.

Before I had formally come out to my parents, I remember talking with a friend about his coming out experience. He told me that he'd decided to come out to his mom one evening after dinner. So he'd sat her down and confidently told her that he was gay. She'd looked at him with love in her eyes and said that she would love him no matter who he was. Then they took a shot together.

While I was happy that he had such a positive outcome, I knew that my parents wouldn't react the same way as his mother did. Based off what I knew about the religion I'd grown up with, I ascertained that my coming out would cause quite a disruption to the family household. And I was right. The news I shared wasn't greeted with acceptance but defiance. Knowing that didn't make it easier, but it took the shock factor out of the equation. Because of that, I was prepared to stand my ground. The first time I came out, I obliged in following what my parents thought was right for me. The second time I came out, I was confident in going my own direction.

As per the story that makes up this book, telling my family that I was gay caused a lot of discord between them and me. It was a horrible burden to bear, but it was better than hiding all of my life. The exhaustion that comes with hiding is as unbearable as the tribulations of not being accepted. But by coming out, I no longer had to live a lie. No one should have to hide because of their sexuality. Being hidden is like not being seen at all. And that's a lonely place to be. My family and I still don't agree on certain issues surrounding my sexual identity. But the beautiful thing now is that when we talk about it, there are no more arguments. They are willing to be open and to listen. And that is a giant leap forward.

You Can't Care What People Think or Say

This is a hard one because we all care what people think of us, to some degree. For those of us who are people-pleasers, the battle is that much harder. People will always have their own opinions and, more often than not, share them with or without your consent. They're going to be expressed, no matter what. So you have to be ready to let those things roll off of your back. This isn't to say you need to be rude, but you take what they say with a grain of salt and you move on. No one is living your life but you. And with that, no one knows your struggles like you do.

We're all experts in other people's problems. We love to judge. And believe me: the judgements will come. But those who have the most to say are also those who have the most to hide. It's easy to judge from the sidelines, but it's completely different when you're playing the game.

Focus on being your authentic self, and the rest will fall into place. Never forget that you're a role model for someone. Not being true to yourself is robbing them of the very reason they look up to you. It's scary to think that people look up to us, but you're pretty cool; so, naturally, others will want to be like you.

Sometimes Letting Go Is the Painful but Only Answer

I'm in no way advocating you disown or leave your family. However, if they aren't willing to accept you or you find yourself in an unsafe environment, then you have to find the strength to remove yourself from that kind of toxic wasteland.

I have met so many men, even in their late twenties and thirties, who are still closeted because they don't want to make trouble and disappoint their families. I understand the importance of family and that the relationship is paramount. But I feel pained for these individuals who are living a lie, exhausted.

I met a friend many years ago when I first came out. Over time, we developed a wonderful friendship, and he shared with me some of his story. He explained to me his background, which was frighteningly similar to mine, although he came from a much stricter circle of evangelicals. He did the Christian thing, went to Bible college, met the girl, brought her home (to his parents delight), popped the question and married his best friend before God and everyone else. He shared with me that he had struggled with homosexuality throughout his teenage years and college. He was told over and over that it was wrong until it was etched into his mind and thinking. He thought that marrying a good Christian woman would help relieve him of this sin, so he did.

And this is a common theme among those who grow up gay with an evangelical background. I have certainly entertained these same thoughts. A short time into his marriage, he realized that he had succumbed to erroneous thinking. He was as gay as the day is long. And there was no changing that. Fortunately, he opted to have a conversation with his wife and pour his heart out to her. She really was his best friend. And while the news broke her heart, she graciously put her arms around him and accepted this news with unconditional love. It wouldn't have been fair to stay married, so they came to a mutual agreement to divorce. They are now both in happy, committed relationships with the people they deserve to love and who deserve their love.

I also have many friends who find themselves in similar situations as the guy mentioned above; however, these friends haven't come to the place to have that conversation with the people who deserve it the most. And that's completely up to them. I hope that one day they can find the contentment they deserve so that they can start actually living and stop pretending.

You deserve to live in happiness. You deserve to be the exact person you were created to be, no matter whether that checks a man-made god box or not. At some point, you have to live your own life. And if your family wants to celebrate with you on that journey, then that's amazing. But if they don't, then you don't deserve to be held hostage emotionally for the sake of their happiness. Personal suffering is too great a price to pay to keep others content.

I learned that if you're unhappy about a situation in your life, then change it. We have the power to change our lives if we really want to. Sometimes we have to be patient, but as long as we're willing to have patience, then we will find our way eventually. It doesn't always come easily. We must work for our accomplishments. I remember many times driving down the country roads that led to my parents' house imagining myself as a mainline flight attendant. As I drove, I would put myself in the aircraft, dressing myself in the uniform and making up scenes in my head of how I would interact with the passengers. I thrived in my fantasy. One day I would get off of that mountain, and I did.

I learned that through our victories and failures that we learn who we are. I believe I'm better off now than I was when I first started. I'm better off because I failed miserably. My experiences shaped my decisions and influenced my thoughts.

My worldview served as a catalyst to bring me through the tortures of my sexual journey. I never imagined I would go through the things I went through, but in a serious way, I wouldn't change anything. After all, I wouldn't be writing this had the preceding events not happened the way that they did. And the impact was so great that my life hung in the balance. Through it all, God's grace brought me above the limitations I put on myself, and saved me from the pit I dug for myself. My experiences were tools to build a better structure that I call my life, my morals, my boundaries, and my thinking.

One of the most influential things I learned through my journey is that I'm good enough. I'm worthy enough. And the truth is that God doesn't want perfection. I believe that God's standard is much lower than what man has labeled as God's standard. God knows who we are and what we can handle. He wants us to be real. The problem wasn't with me—it was with the system that no man could satisfy. No one will ever be perfect, so perfection shouldn't be the goal. What does matter is that we try and keep trying to do our best. God meets us where we are. We don't have to earn an award to know God. He takes us as we are, no matter what. Love is the name of the game. I believe that if we focused more on loving and understanding others rather than tallying up how many God boxes we check, we would reap much more acceptance and positive change in our communities.

Above all, my hope is that you find the strength to be open about who you are. You don't deserve to fade into the background. I want you to live the life of abundance because it's available to you. You're innately given the strength you need to fight all of your battles. You are equipped with the tools you need to live the life you dream of. The one thing I urge you not to do is give up. Don't quit; your future is full of wondrous possibilities.

Acknowledgements

First, a big shout out to Mattie who was my solid rock during some of the darkest times of my life. She uplifted me in ways she will never know; I can't speak enough accolades to express how truly wonderful she is. And I can't wait for her to marry her incredible fiancé, Greg. I also want to thank Sam Horn for unforgettable moments in nursing school and beyond. I will always remember during the beginning of our friendship when we went to a coffee shop near the nursing school. We talked about our dating lives, and I told Sam in a very serious tone that I was not gay, but straight. She gave me a look of pure shock. Then I said, "Nah, I am just kidding." And she let out a sigh of relief.

I would like to thank Dr. Kim Amer, my nursing professor who taught nursing theory, which is what eventually inspired my master's thesis in music therapy. Little did I know that I would continue to work on this project with her until it would get published in a nursing journal. Dr. Amer believed in me, pushed me to be better, and has served as my mentor over the past several years. Words cannot describe how grateful I am to know her, and I look forward to future collaborations with her.

Lori Bennett was a guiding light during my time at American Airlines and continues to be to this day. She accepted me for exactly who I was without question. After I met Lori, I met Allison and Kathleen on a work trip to London, England. We made it a point to get together once every couple of months for lunch. These women were good to me by providing a safe space, and I'll never forget their kindness. Until our next brunch, ladies!

Ariel Gray was special to me because she allowed me to be myself, quirks and all. Her response when I came out to her was a very familiar,

"I know. I was just waiting for you to tell me." I will always love her and value the amazing woman she is.

I want to thank the nurses at Weiss Hospital and the two staff members previously mentioned at the psych hospital for taking care of me in my darkest hour. Your knowledge and expertise saved me, and I am indebted to you. I also want to thank my nursing family on liver/kidney transplant at Northwestern. You all made the start of my nursing career extraordinary, and I am exuberant I can call you all friends.

To Courtney Williams and David Calderon, two of the best roommates a person could ask for, thank you for welcoming me into your lives and creating wonderful memories with me. Thanks for putting up with me through the years and showing me what true friends look like.

I want to thank Ryan and all of my friends at UVA who helped make my transition flawless. I would not be where I am today without you. So, thank you for believing in me and accepting me with open arms. You mean the world to me.

I would be remiss if I ended this chapter without mentioning my family. I know that we have had our differences, but the point of this book is not to place blame. I will never be able to repay the sacrifices you all made to be there for me after my attempt. I find it a bit ironic that our differences, which once divided us, have brought us closer, in a way. We no longer avoid conversations about my being gay, but choose to listen to each other and learn from each other. I want to thank my parents for always loving me no matter what. Though there have been bumps along the way, I am blessed to have you, and I love you all very much.

Thanks to everyone who worked on this book and inspired me throughout the process.